STAR TREK™

THE BOOK OF LISTS

CHIP CARTER

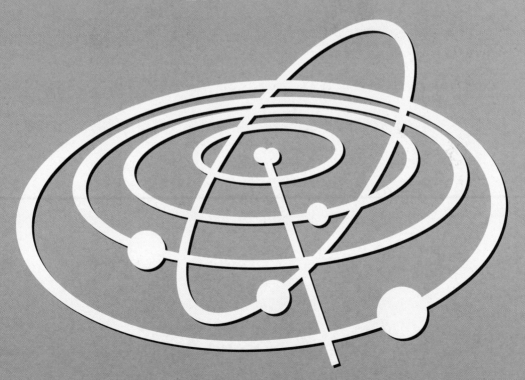

HARPER DESIGN
An Imprint of HarperCollins Publishers

TO MY IMZADI, FERNANDO GUZMAN —
YOU MAKE THE CONTINUING MISSION
OF LIFE FUN AND BRAND-NEW
EACH AND EVERY STARDATE —
I LOVE YOU!

AND

TO WRITER & ACTRESS MELANIE RASKIN —
I TRULY WOULD NOT HAVE COME THIS FAR
AS A WRITER WITHOUT YOUR
LOVE AND SUPPORT!
QAPLA'!

Star Trek: The Book of Lists is produced by becker&mayer! Book Producers, Bellevue, Washington.
www.beckermayer.com

HarperCollins books may be purchased for educational, business, or sales promotional use. For
information please e-mail the Special Markets Department at SPsales@harpercollins.com.

First published in 2017 by
Harper Design
An Imprint of HarperCollins*Publishers*
195 Broadway
New York, NY 10007
Tel: (212) 207-7000
Fax: (855) 746-6023
harperdesign@harpercollins.com
www.hc.com

Distributed throughout the world by:
HarperCollins*Publishers*
195 Broadway
New York, NY 10007

Designer: Scott Richardson
Editor: Paul Ruditis
Production coordinator: Olivia Holmes

Library of Congress Cataloging-in-Publication Data is available upon request.

ISBN 978-0-06-268588-9

First Printing, 2017

Printed and bound in China

Image credits: Page 156 ©Ryan J. Thompson/ Shutterstock.com; Page 198 ©AF archive/ Alamy Stock Photo; Page 200 ©AF archive/
Alamy Stock Photo; Page 201 ©AF archive/ Alamy Stock Photo; Page 214 ©Valeria Fefilova/ Shutterstock.com; Page 217 Image
Courtesy National Aeronautics and Space Administration; Page 218 ©White House Photo/ Alamy Stock Photo.

All design elements provided by Shutterstock.com.

CONTENTS

INTRODUCTION

When *Star Trek* first aired on September 8, 1966, no one—not creator Gene Roddenberry, the network, or even the first enthusiastic fans of the show—could have predicted the pop-culture phenomenon that had begun.

Star Trek: The Original Series (TOS) depicting the adventures of Captain Kirk, Spock, and Dr. McCoy on board the *U.S.S. Enterprise* NCC-1701 may have only lasted three seasons before being canceled but the fans and their love of the show refused to let it die. As *Star Trek* conventions sprang up, *Star Trek: The Animated Series* (TAS) appeared on Saturday mornings, featuring the voice talents of the original cast. Several years later, the first film paved the way for twelve more motion pictures.

Some twenty years after the launch of the original show, a bold new series aired in syndication—*Star Trek: The Next Generation* (TNG). Set seventy-five years after Kirk and Spock's time, the new show broadened the universe as Captain Picard, Commander Riker, and Data and crew traveled the Galaxy in the *U.S.S. Enterprise* NCC-1701D. The success of the show led to more spin-offs in *Star Trek: Deep Space Nine* (DS9), *Star Trek: Voyager* (VGR), and the prequels *Star Trek: Enterprise* (ENT) and (the most recent) *Star Trek: Discovery* (DSC). Feature films also transitioned from the TOS cast to the TNG cast, before ending with the last film in 2002. For a few years, the franchise was dormant, until being rebooted in 2009 with a new timeline, new actors playing Kirk, Spock, and crew, and even a surprising guest star from the original *Star Trek*.

While no book could distill over seven hundred hours of programming into just one hundred lists, the following lists include some of the highlights, excitement, and fun of more than fifty years of strange new worlds and new civilizations.

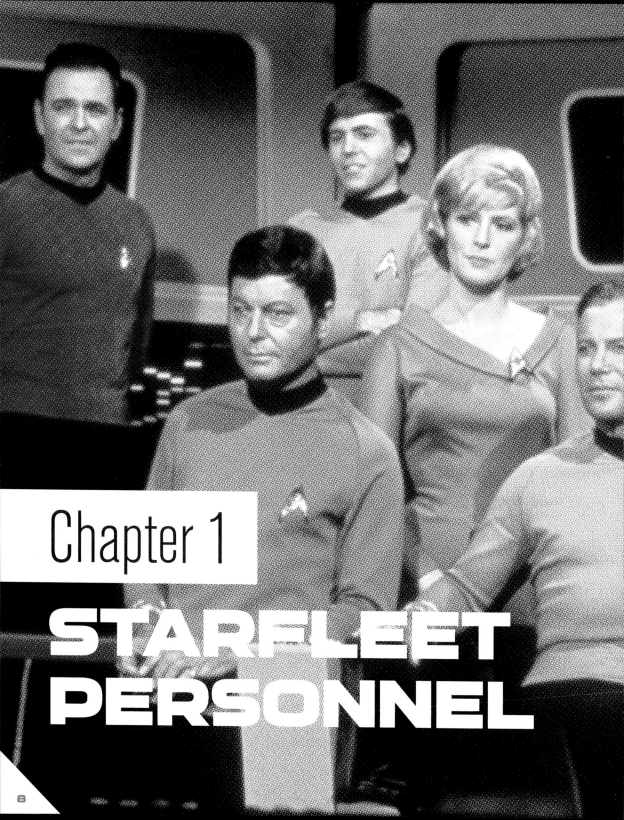

Chapter 1
STARFLEET PERSONNEL

KIRK'S MOST MEMORABLE KISSES

WHILE CAPTAIN JAMES T. KIRK'S MOST LASTING RELATIONSHIP WAS THE ONE WITH HIS SHIP, HE ENJOYED ROMANTIC ENTANGLEMENTS WITH BEAUTIFUL WOMEN ACROSS THE QUADRANTS. SOMETIMES THE WOMEN HE KISSED WERE FLIRTATIOUS AND SOMETIMES THEY WERE DANGEROUS, BUT THEY ALWAYS PROPELLED HIM AT WARP SPEED BACK TO HIS ONE TRUE LOVE: THE *STARSHIP ENTERPRISE*.

Edith Keeler Chasing a maddened Dr. McCoy into Earth's past brought Kirk and Spock into contact with social worker Edith Keeler. Kirk fell deeply in love and Edith kissed him when he saved her from stumbling down the stairs. What he could not save her from was history; if she didn't die as she was supposed to, the Nazis would win World War II. Kirk had to keep himself and a restored McCoy from saving her when she was hit by a truck.

TOS "THE CITY ON THE EDGE OF FOREVER"

Lenore Karidian Kirk's first kiss with the actress was forestalled when they discovered the body of his old friend, Dr. Thomas Leighton, while the *Enterprise* conveyed her acting troupe to their next destination. The troupe also included Lenore's father, the suspected criminal Kodos the Executioner. Kirk romanced Lenore, hoping to uncover the truth behind her father's identity. Sadly, Lenore knew of her father's past and was killing anyone who may suspect, making their actual kiss almost fatal.

TOS "THE CONSCIENCE OF THE KING"

Marlena Moreau While trapped in a "mirror" universe where the Federation was an evil empire, Kirk encountered the seductive Lt. Marlena Moreau, who shared the alternate Captain Kirk's lust for power. When she threatened to leave the ship, Kirk kissed her passionately and changed her mind. Back in his own universe, Kirk was surprised again to see that his universe's version of Lieutenant Moreau now served aboard his ship.

TOS "MIRROR MIRROR"

Yeoman Rand Though their professional relationship was always tinged with an attraction (during one crisis on the bridge, she even *held hands* with Kirk), their only kiss was not consensual. A savage duplicate of Kirk created in a transporter accident tried to force himself on Rand. She got away, and after the duplicate was gone, Rand and Kirk managed to repair their relationship.

TOS "THE ENEMY WITHIN"

Areel Shaw Though Kirk's former lover had not seen him in "four years, seven months, and an odd number of days," Lieutenant Areel Shaw had mixed feelings about meeting with Kirk again. She was now the prosecuting officer in the court-martial against him. Ultimately, Kirk was proven innocent and Shaw thought "it would cause a complete breakdown of discipline if a lowly lieutenant kissed a starship captain on the bridge of his ship" before they decided to take that risk.

TOS "COURT-MARTIAL"

Shahna Kirk was kidnapped by the mysterious Providers of the planet Triskelion to fight in their combat games. At first, the captain's stern, green-haired drill thrall, Shahna, seemed uninterested in anything but combat. That changed after he spared Shahna's life in the games and earned his freedom. Kirk was unable to take her with him, but he kissed Shahna farewell, leaving her to "learn and watch the lights in the sky."

TOS "THE GAMESTERS OF TRISKELION"

Andrea The android Andrea, built by Dr. Roger Korby, first kissed Kirk, then slapped him when Dr. Korby wanted to prove she had no emotion. However, when Kirk and Andrea kissed again, she began to feel confused and emotional—perhaps proving she had been built too well. When she professed her love for Dr. Korby (now an android himself) he destroyed them both, overwhelmed by the loss of his humanity and the emergence of hers.

TOS "WHAT ARE LITTLE GIRLS MADE OF?"

Lieutenant Uhura Perhaps the most famous of Kirk's kisses was most notable for its real-world significance. Captured by the telekinetic Platonians and forced to entertain their captors, Kirk and Uhura were made to kiss. This was the first time a scripted interracial kiss had been seen on television and was considered daring for a network show during the 1960s.

TOS "PLATO'S STEPCHILDREN"

Other memorable kisses include Miramanee in "The Paradise Syndrome," Elaan in "Elaan of Troyius," and Drusilla in "Bread and Circuses."

FASCINATING, FEELINGS

While many assume Vulcans have no emotions at all, this is incorrect. Thousands of years ago, their violent passions nearly wiped out their society. The philosopher Surak developed a culture of devotion to logic that saved them. No matter how shameful it may be to Vulcan society, however, those emotions sometimes surface. For most Vulcans, it is only during *Pon Farr*, the secretive mating rituals that happen once every seven years. But for Mr. Spock, the half-human science officer on the *Enterprise*, his encounters with various phenomena often caused cracks in his logical facade. These are just a few of the storylines that allowed Leonard Nimoy to tap into the emotions he was regularly forced to suppress while playing the stoic Vulcan.

"The Cage"/"The Menagerie" While under the command of the *Enterprise*'s former captain, Christopher Pike, Spock appeared to not yet have achieved the emotional control he would later display. As part of the landing party to Talos IV, Spock openly smiled when he and Pike discovered singing flowers.

"Yesteryear" (TAS) When Spock traveled back in time, he met his younger self still struggling with his Human emotions. After being teased by other Vulcan youths, the angry young Spock attacked the other boys. The two Spocks journeyed to the desert for a rite of maturity when Spock's pet *sehlat* was mortally injured. Though upset, the young Spock made the difficult decision to let the *sehlat* die with dignity and chose the Vulcan way of logic.

"This Side of Paradise" Exposure to Omicron spores caused a euphoric state, and Spock enjoyed a short time of bliss with former acquaintance Leila Kalomi. Kirk found that intense emotion broke the plant's euphoric spell, and he was able to anger Spock enough to let his Vulcan logic reassert itself.

"The Devil in the Dark" When Spock mind-melded with the injured Horta, its grief and pain brought Spock to tears.

"Plato's Stepchildren" The Platonians used their psychokinetic powers to force the crew of the *Enterprise* to perform numerous humiliating acts for their amusement. Spock finally kissed Chapel, who had pined for him for a while, though it was not the way she had wished it would have happened.

"Amok Time" Though Spock tried to resist the mating urges of the *Pon farr*, his "blood fever" boiled to the point he even threw a bowl of soup at Nurse Chapel. Once he returned to Vulcan and participated in the *kal-if-fee* challenge, the emotional imbalance restored itself. Spock mistakenly thought he'd killed Captain Kirk during the challenge, and when he saw Kirk alive, a brief smile flashed across his face.

"The Naked Time" As members of the crew succumbed to a virus that lowered their inhibitions, Spock was infected but attempted to regain logical control before weeping for his mother. It was not until Captain Kirk physically and emotionally lashed out at him that Spock, who watched his captain fall victim to the disease, began to regain control of his emotions and could help save the ship.

"All Our Yesterdays" Thrown into the distant past and altered at the cellular level, Spock began to revert to the ways of his barbarian Vulcan ancestors. He ate meat, kissed the time-exiled Zarabeth, and attacked McCoy. Once they returned to the present, he was able to regain his logical mindset.

Star Trek: The Motion Picture After failing to undergo the *kohlinar* ritual designed to purge the last of his emotions, Spock reunited with the *Enterprise* crew more distant than ever. He performed a mind-meld with the alien V'Ger, which knocked him unconscious. Once awake, he commented sadly on his newfound understanding that the machine entity could never comprehend even simple feelings like the friendship he had found with Kirk. He later wept for V'Ger's emptiness in its search for meaning.

"I'M A DOCTOR, NOT A . . ."

While exploring the final frontier, the *U.S.S. Enterprise* senior medical officer, Dr. Leonard "Bones" McCoy, was often called upon to heal or save patients, both Human and otherwise. As gifted a physician and surgeon as he was, when confronted with some baffling problem outside of medical expertise, time and time again, he would emphatically tell Kirk what he was not.

- After Kirk found that McCoy had kept him unaware of a red alert so he could finally complete his quarterly physical:
  "What am I, a doctor or a moon shuttle conductor?" . . . . TOS "THE CORBOMITE MANEUVER"

- When asked to heal an injured silicon-based life-form, the Horta:
  "I'm a doctor, not a bricklayer." . . . . TOS "THE DEVIL IN THE DARK"

- When asked if he wanted to see Edith Keeler's strange new friends:
  "I'm a surgeon, not a psychiatrist." . . . . TOS "THE CITY ON THE EDGE OF FOREVER"

- When asked if he'd heard of the doomsday machine:
  "I'm a doctor, not a mechanic." . . . . TOS "THE DOOMSDAY MACHINE"

- When the pregnant Eleen demanded that only McCoy could help her climb to a cave:
  "I'm a doctor, not an escalator." . . . . TOS "FRIDAY'S CHILD"

- When realizing he was supposed to help Scotty find a way back to their own universe:
  "I'm a doctor, not an engineer." . . . . TOS "MIRROR MIRROR"

- When arguing with Spock over whether Humans should be so far underground:
  "I'm a doctor, not a coal miner." . . . . TOS "THE EMPATH"

In the *Kelvin* Timeline, Dr. McCoy added more colorful language to his famous catchphrase.

- When discussing the possibility that Nero's ship had traveled through time:
  "Damn it, man, I'm a doctor, not a physicist." . . . . STAR TREK (2009)

- On being asked if he could replicate his activation of a torpedo:
  "Damn it, man, I'm a doctor, not a torpedo technician." . . . . STAR TREK INTO DARKNESS

- As he was reluctantly being beamed away with Spock to sever the connection between drone ships:
  "Damn it, Jim. I'm a doctor not a—" (He dematerialized before he could finish the sentence.)
  STAR TREK BEYOND

"I'M ALSO A DOCTOR . . ."

As the *Star Trek* universe expanded and viewers saw more and more medical personnel, other doctors began to pay homage to McCoy's famous catchphrase.

"I'm a doctor, not a botanist." Bashir . . . . DS9 "THE WIRE"

"I'm a doctor, not an historian." Bashir . . . . .DS9 "TRIALS AND TRIBBLE-ATIONS"

"I'm a doctor, not a bartender." The Doctor . . . . VGR "TWISTED"

"I'm a doctor, not a counterinsurgent." The Doctor . . . . VGR "BASICS, PART II"

"I'm a doctor, not a zookeeper." The Doctor . . . . VGR "LIFE LINE"

"I'm a doctor, not a commando." EMH Mark II . . . . VGR "MESSAGE IN A BOTTLE"

"I'm a physician, not an engineer." Phlox . . . . ENT "DOCTOR'S ORDERS"

"I'm a doctor, not a doorstop." EMH Mark I on the *U.S.S. Enterprise* NCC-1701-E . . . . . STAR TREK: FIRST CONTACT

Other characters then staked their own claims on what they were and were not:

"I'm a security chief, not a combat pilot." Odo . . . . DS9 "VORTEX"

"I'm a magazine editor, I'm not a crusader." Douglas Pabst (Odo) . . . . DS9 "FAR BEYOND THE STARS"

"I am a warrior, not a murderer!" Worf . . . . DS9 "BROKEN LINK"

"I'm a pilot, Harry, not a doctor!" Paris . . . . VGR "MESSAGE IN A BOTTLE"

"I'm an engineer, not a costume designer." Torres . . . . VGR "VIRTUOSO"

THE MIRACLE WORKER

FROM "ABERDEEN PUB CRAWLER" TO "MIRACLE WORKER," COMMANDER MONTGOMERY SCOTT SERVED ON ELEVEN SHIPS OVER A FIFTY-YEAR CAREER. DURING HIS TIME ABOARD THE *U.S.S. ENTERPRISE*, KIRK AND THE SENIOR STAFF BEGAN TO CALL SCOTTY A MIRACLE WORKER AS HE COULD REPAIR ALMOST ANYTHING IN RECORD TIME—THOUGH YEARS LATER, HE WOULD ADMIT THAT HE GENERALLY PADDED HIS REPAIR ESTIMATES BY A FACTOR OF FOUR. SOME OF HIS GREATEST MIRACLES INCLUDE:

"Mudd's Women" Beamed Harry Mudd and his three female associates aboard after three of the ship's lithium crystal circuits were destroyed.

"The Enemy Within" Assisted in modifying the transporter to reintegrate the good and evil versions of Kirk.

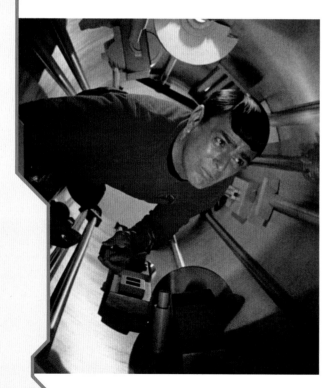

"The Naked Time" Performed a cold restart of the warp engines in under ten minutes with the assistance of Spock's untested intermix formula.

"The Galileo Seven" Powered the *Galileo* shuttle using hand phasers.

"The Doomsday Machine" Rigged the *U.S.S. Constellation* to explode in order to destroy the planet killer, then repaired the *Enterprise* transporters to beam Kirk safely back from the *Constellation*.

"Mirror, Mirror" Altered the *I.S.S. Enterprise* transporters to allow Kirk, Uhura, McCoy, and himself to leave the Mirror Universe.

"That Which Survives" Manually shut off the fuel flow from the matter/antimatter engines with only a magnetic probe.

Star Trek III: The Search for Spock Automated the *U.S.S. Enterprise* to run with a skeleton crew, then sabotaged the *U.S.S. Excelsior*'s transwarp drive.

Star Trek IV: The Voyage Home Repaired a bird-of-prey to take the crew from Vulcan to Earth, despite having trouble reading Klingon.

"Relics" (TNG) Retired engineer Scott kept himself alive in a transporter buffer pattern for almost seventy-five years.

THE RUSSIAN COSMONAUT

LIST #6

Ensign Pavel Andreievich Chekov was an enthusiastic ensign when he joined the crew of the *U.S.S. Enterprise*. He eventually became the navigator and weapons officer, as well as a relief science officer. He later was promoted to first officer on the *U.S.S. Reliant*, before rejoining his former crew on the *Enterprise*. Throughout his life he has been fiercely proud of his Russian heritage, and his sometimes unreliable version of history claimed many events, inventions, literature, and beverages were of Russian origin, including:

"The Apple" The Garden of Eden was apparently located outside Moscow.

"Friday's Child" The famous saying, "Fool me once, shame on you . . ." was invented in Russia.

"Who Mourns for Adonais?" The Cheshire Cat in *Alice's Adventures in Wonderland* was derived from a story of a disappearing cat from Minsk.

"The Trouble with Tribbles" More than any other episode, Chekov was feeling the love for Mother Russia when he noted…

Scotch was invented by a little old lady from Leningrad. (Also mentioned in *Star Trek Beyond*)

Quadrotriticale was not invented in Canada, but in Russia.

Ivan Burkoff, rather than John Burke, mapped the area of space around Sherman's Planet.

Peter the Great once faced a similar dilemma as the Federation and Klingons in dealing with Sherman's Planet.

Star Trek VI: The Undiscovered Country Cinderella was a Russian fable.

"I, Mudd" Surprisingly, he described Planet Mudd as being even better than Leningrad!

HAILING FREQUENCIES OPEN

LIEUTENANT NYOTA UHURA WAS A MULTITALENTED OFFICER. THOUGH HER FOCUS WAS COMMUNICATIONS, HER BACKGROUND IN TECHNOLOGY ALLOWED HER TO OCCASIONALLY TAKE OVER SPOCK'S SCIENCE STATION, THE NAVIGATION STATION, AND EVEN COMMAND OF THE *ENTERPRISE*. HOWEVER, SHE IS BEST REMEMBERED FOR THE MANY SHIPS, ALIENS, AND PLANETS SHE OPENED THE SHIP'S HAILING FREQUENCIES FOR WITH HER SIGNATURE LINE OF DIALOGUE, INCLUDING:

Balok, Fesarius
TOS "THE CORBOMITE MANEUVER"

Doctor Adams, Tantalus Penal Colony
TOS "DAGGER OF THE MIND"

Romulan Commander, Romulan ship
TOS "BALANCE OF TERROR"

Nomad
TOS "THE CHANGELING"

***U.S.S. Lexington* (signal blocked by M-5)**
TOS "THE ULTIMATE COMPUTER"

Sigma Draconis vessel (no response)
TOS "SPOCK'S BRAIN"

Melkotian buoy (no response)
TOS "SPECTRE OF THE GUN"

***U.S.S. Defiant* (no response)**
TOS "THE THOLIAN WEB"

Klingon vessel
TOS "ELAAN OF TROYIUS"

Lokai's shuttle (no response)
TOS "LET THAT BE YOUR LAST BATTLEFIELD"

Paradise City, Nimbus III
STAR TREK V: THE FINAL FRONTIER

Chancellor Gorkon, *Kronos One*
STAR TREK VI: THE UNDISCOVERED COUNTRY

SWASHBUCKLING SULU

THE HELMSMAN OF THE *U.S.S. ENTERPRISE* WAS NOT ONLY AN EXPERT PILOT, HE WAS ADEPT AT HAND-TO-HAND COMBAT AND PROFICIENT WITH SWORDS AND OTHER WEAPONS. THE FUTURE CAPTAIN OF THE *U.S.S. EXCELSIOR* WAS GENERALLY CALM AND COLLECTED BUT NEVER HESITATED TO SHOW OFF HIS STYLE DURING A FIGHT. SOME OF THE MORE DARING MOVES SULU DISPLAYED INCLUDE:

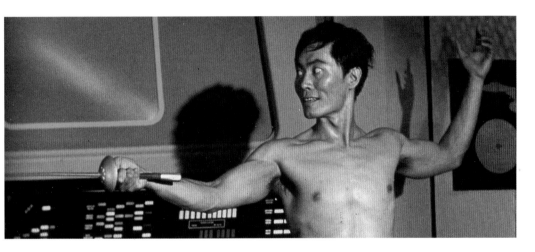

"The Naked Time" When the Psi 2000 infection attacked Sulu, he wielded a rapier and menaced other crewmen as he imagined himself as a musketeer.

"Shore Leave" Sulu's excitement at finding an ancient Earth police revolver dimmed when a samurai warrior attacked him and Sulu's phaser had no effect.

Star Trek VI: The Undiscovered Country Finally captain of his own ship, Sulu traded in the fisticuffs for starship tactics as he helped the crew of the *Enterprise*-A defeat General Chang in the Khitomer system.

"The Infinite Vulcan" (TAS) While on the planet Phylos, a humanoid plant attacked Sulu and he performed a judo throw that Kirk later wanted to learn.

"Operation—Annihilate!" Sulu was one of four bridge crew that helped pin down the much-stronger Spock when the Vulcan was maddened by pain caused by neural parasites.

"Mirror, Mirror" The version of Sulu from the Mirror Universe bore scars from previous fights, but he was no match for the Kirk from the prime universe.

Star Trek III: The Search for Spock When a much-larger security guard insulted Sulu's size, the officer promptly flipped the man over. After knocking him out, Sulu famously said, "Don't call me 'Tiny.'"

Star Trek V: The Final Frontier Sulu helped lead the charge to save three ambassadors being held hostage by Sybok on Nimbus III, at one point rolling off a horse and shooting out a searchlight.

BEING THE CHIEF MEDICAL OFFICER FOR A STARSHIP OR STARBASE WITH A COMPLEMENT OF UP TO A THOUSAND CREWMEMBERS PUTS HUGE DEMANDS ON A DOCTOR'S TIME. THE CHIEF MEDICAL OFFICER WOULD NEVER BE ABLE TO TREAT AN ENTIRE SHIP'S WORTH OF AILMENTS RANGING FROM RIGELIAN FEVER TO TEPLAN BLIGHT WITHOUT ANY ASSISTANCE. FORTUNATELY, THESE MEDICAL PROFESSIONALS STEP UP AND ALLOW A DOCTOR ENOUGH TIME TO GET IN A GAME OF HOLOGRAPHIC GOLF ONCE IN A WHILE.

Nurse Chapel Dr. McCoy's primary support staff during his tenure as chief medical officer of the *U.S.S. Enterprise* later became a doctor and returned to the *Enterprise* after its refit. During the "whale probe" attack on Earth, she coordinated relief efforts at Starfleet Headquarters.

TOS/*STAR TREK IV: THE VOYAGE HOME*

Dr. Dehner The psychiatrist on board the *U.S.S. Enterprise* in the life sciences division once published a thesis on the ESP capabilities of psionic beings.

TOS "WHERE NO MAN HAS GONE BEFORE"

EMH Mark II The "improved" model of the Emergency Medical Hologram unwillingly welcomed *Voyager*'s EMH aboard the *U.S.S. Prometheus* after it had been hijacked. The Mark II was condescending toward the prior model, but nonetheless helped him fight off the Romulans and gained a grudging respect for the Mark I.

VGR "MESSAGE IN A BOTTLE"

Tom Paris The helm officer aboard the *U.S.S. Voyager* possessed a limited background in biochemistry, but it was enough for Captain Janeway to choose him to be a medical assistant to the EMH and field medic after the ship was stranded in the Delta Quadrant. While Paris grew more capable at the job over the years, he never relished it, preferring to fly the ship than to administer hyposprays.

VGR

Dr. M'Benga Another member of Kirk's crew, M'Benga served his medical internship on Vulcan, and was aware of best practices for treating members of that species, such as slapping them to bring them out of a healing trance.

TOS "A PRIVATE LITTLE WAR"

Dr. Katherine Pulaski The noted heart surgeon served as chief medical officer aboard the *U.S.S. Enterprise*-D during the time Dr. Beverly Crusher accepted the position of head of Starfleet Medical. Pulaski transferred off the *Enterprise* prior to Dr. Crusher's return.

TNG

Elizabeth Cutler The exobiologist serving under the command of Captain Jonathan Archer aboard the *Enterprise* NX-01 began to assist Dr. Phlox as a trainee medic and also developed feelings for the Denobulan doctor. When Phlox told Cutler he was already married, she took it in stride and insisted they would remain friends.

ENT

Dr. Selar The Vulcan physician who served aboard the *U.S.S. Enterprise*-D was only seen once onscreen, though her character was referenced many times throughout the run of *Star Trek: The Next Generation*.

Kes For the three years Kes was aboard the *U.S.S. Voyager*, the Ocampan worked closely with the Doctor in sickbay, training under him and assisting as his nurse. She was also interested in airponics and established a garden in one of *Voyager*'s cargo bays.

VGR

Nurse Ogawa As Dr. Crusher's right hand in sickbay, Alyssa Ogawa worked her way from ensign to lieutenant by the time the *Enterprise*-E was commissioned. Ogawa was discreet and loyal, and even risked her career at one point to help Dr. Crusher with a forbidden autopsy to prove a scientist's theory.

TNG "SUSPICIONS"/"ALL GOOD THINGS . . ."/ *STAR TREK: FIRST CONTACT*

DIPLOMATIC RELATIONS

In the future, the four quadrants of the Galaxy enjoy peace . . . most of the time. Nevertheless, there are always skirmishes, misunderstandings, and other situations that call for diplomacy. Some of the top diplomats in the Galaxy are prepared to handle any intergalactic incidents.

Sarek Spock's father was a member of the Federation Council, as well as a legendary ambassador. He was involved in such high-profile negotiations as the Khitomer Accords, the Treaty of Alliance between the Federation and Klingons, and the ninety-three years of preliminary discussions with the Legarans.

TOS "JOURNEY TO BABEL"

Lwaxana Troi Daughter of the Fifth House, holder of the Sacred Chalice of Rixx, heir to the Holy Rings of Betazed, Counselor Deanna Troi's mother was as grand and eccentric as her exotic titles. While she was flamboyant, her shrewd mind and her telepathic abilities made her a formidable ambassador.

TNG/DS9

K'Ehleyr Half Human and half Klingon, K'Ehleyr was a special emissary tasked with reintegrating the crew of a Klingon sleeper ship unaware of the peace treaty between the Federation and the Klingon Empire.

TNG "THE EMISSARY"/"REUNION"

Shras The ambassador from Andoria, Shras was also aboard the *U.S.S. Enterprise* as it traveled to Babel to debate the Coridan issue.

TOS "JOURNEY TO BABEL"

Gav Brash and aggressive, like so many Tellarites, the ambassador confronted Sarek on Vulcan's position on admitting Coridan, a dilithium-rich planet, to the Federation.

TOS "JOURNEY TO BABEL"

Spock After years of service in Starfleet, Spock finally followed in his father's footsteps and became an ambassador. He was first a special envoy to Qo'noS and then a secret envoy to Romulus in an attempt to unify the Vulcan and Romulan people.

STAR TREK VI: THE UNDISCOVERED COUNTRY/ TNG "UNIFICATION"

Commodore Robert April The first captain of the *U.S.S. Enterprise*, Robert April served as a Federation ambassador-at-large for twenty years, before reaching Starfleet's mandatory retirement age.

TAS "THE COUNTER-CLOCK INCIDENT"

Odan The symbiont from the Trill homeworld had been joined to a host who became attracted to Dr. Beverly Crusher while he was on a mission to mediate between the two moons.

TNG "THE HOST"

GALACTIC GLADIATORS

IN THE TWENTY-THIRD CENTURY, CAPTAIN KIRK OFTEN TOOK MATTERS INTO HIS OWN HANDS . . . LITERALLY. THE *ENTERPRISE* CAPTAIN WASN'T AVERSE TO BARE-KNUCKLE BRAWLING, OR SPARRING WITH WEAPONS. STARFLEET OFFICERS OF THE TWENTY-FOURTH CENTURY USUALLY TRIED TO REASON WITH HOSTILE OPPONENTS. SOMETIMES, THOUGH, THE ONLY RESORT IS THE LAST ONE. SOME GALACTIC HEAVYWEIGHT CHAMPIONSHIPS INCLUDE:

Kirk vs. the Gorn Captain on Cestus III
Winner: Kirk, by a homemade cannon.
TOS "ARENA"

Kirk vs Khan in engineering
Winner: Kirk, by a club-like handle.
TOS "SPACE SEED"

Kirk vs. Spock on Vulcan
Winner: Spock, by a dose of tri-ox compound.
TOS "AMOK TIME"

Picard vs. Picard in the vineyard
Winner: Jean-Luc, by an emotional breakthrough.
TNG "FAMILY"

Picard vs. Nausicaans at Starbase Earhart
Winner: Nausicaans, by a large knife.
TNG "TAPESTRY"

Janeway vs macrovirus in corridor
Winner: Janeway, by a sliced tentacle.
VGR "MACROCOSM"

Sisko vs Bajoran officer in ops
Winner: Sisko, by a futuristic needle.
DS9 "DRAMATIS PERSONAE"

Seven vs a Pendari Champion in *tsunkatse* match
Winner: Pendari Champion, by a polaron disruptor.
VGR "TSUNKATSE"

Deep Space 9 crew vs. Klingons in ops
Winner: DS9 crew, by a couple of *bat'leth*s.
DS9 "THE WAY OF THE WARRIOR"

Archer vs. Shran during *Ushaan* duel
Winner: Archer, by half an antenna.
ENT "UNITED"

RED(SHIRT) ALERT

IT BECAME SOMETHING OF A PATTERN DURING THE ORIGINAL *STAR TREK* SERIES: KIRK, SPOCK, AND MCCOY WOULD BEAM DOWN TO A PLANET AND FACE DANGER, AND SOME EXTRA CREWMEN—USUALLY DRESSED IN THE RED SHIRTS THAT DENOTED THAT THEY WORKED FOR THE OPERATIONS DIVISION (MOST OF THE TIME IN THE SECURITY SECTION)—WOULD END UP DYING FROM POISON THORNS, SPEARS, OR CLOUD CREATURES. RED WAS CLEARLY A COLOR TO AVOID, THOUGH IN THE LATER SERIES, GOLD TUNICS REPLACED RED AS THE COLOR FOR THE OPERATIONS DIVISIONS AS WELL AS MUCH OF ITS UNLUCKY LEGACY. STILL, EVEN IN THE TWENTY-FOURTH CENTURY, RED WAS TO BE AVOIDED AT ALL COSTS. THESE ARE SOME OF THE MORE MEMORABLE FALLEN CREWMEMBERS:

Lieutenant Lee Kelso In the second pilot episode, "Where No Man Has Gone Before" the red shirt curse had not yet struck, and Kelso (clad in gold) became the first ancillary crew member with a name to die onscreen, at the hands of the now-godlike Gary Mitchell.

TOS "WHERE NO MAN HAS GONE BEFORE"

Crewman Matthews The *Enterprise* security guard beamed into a cave on Exo III and was promptly pushed off a cliff by the android Ruk, becoming the first official redshirt to die in the franchise. He was quickly joined by Crewman Rayburn in the same episode.

TOS "WHAT ARE LITTLE GIRLS MADE OF?"

Carlisle Nomad disintegrated this crewman along with an unnamed security guard.

TOS "THE CHANGELING"

The TOS episode "The Apple" featured four redshirts killed off one by one in unique ways: Hendorff (poison pod plant); Marple (hit with a club); Mallory (explosive mineral formations); and Kaplan (struck by lightning).

Yeoman Leslie Thompson Unusual deaths plagued the *Enterprise* crew, with this yeoman reduced to a cubic solid and crushed into dust by Rojan.

TOS "BY ANY OTHER NAME"

Lieutenant Galloway Captain Tracey murdered Galloway with a phaser in one of the less exotic deaths of the series.

TOS "THE OMEGA GLORY"

Ensign Wyatt Losira's deadly touch did in this crew member.

TOS "THAT WHICH SURVIVES"

Mr. Leslie One of the longest-surviving TOS redshirts (appearing in close to sixty episodes, including file footage used in the DS9 episode "Trials and Tribble-ations"), Leslie died at the gaseous "hands" of the dikironium cloud creature, but was inexplicably brought back to life and seen later in the same episode. Perhaps the fact he sometimes wore gold helped him with the curse.

TOS "OBSESSION"

Crewman Ramos A hidden Klingon disruptor was the weapon used to kill Ramos.

TNG "HEART OF GLORY"

Haskell The Nagilum experimented with Haskell, causing a cerebral hemorrhage.

TNG "WHERE SILENCE HAS LEASE"

Lieutenant Hawk After being assimilated by the Borg, Worf killed the lieutenant as the newly turned drone tried to stop Picard and him from sabotaging the Borg interplexing beacon.

STAR TREK: FIRST CONTACT

Ensign Aquino A Bajoran religious activist reduced the ensign to organic matter when he discovered the woman attempting to bypass a security module.

DS9 "IN THE HANDS OF THE PROPHETS"

Amaro Elim Garak killed this unfortunate soul while the simple tailor was under the influence of psychotropic drugs he came in contact with on Empok Nor.

DS9 "EMPOK NOR"

Lieutenant Commander Cavit and Lieutenant Stadi Members of Captain Janeway's bridge crew on *U.S.S. Voyager*'s first mission were killed when a displacement wave threw the ship 70,000 light-years from the Badlands.

VGR "CARETAKER"

Ensign Dern A devolved crew member broke Dern's spinal column in three places.

TNG "GENESIS"

Sito Jaxa This junior member of the crew died while on an undercover mission trying to help a Cardassian defector.

TNG "LOWER DECKS"

M. Forbes Like many of the MACO (Military Assault Command Operations) personnel that served on *Enterprise* NX-01, Forbes died in battle with the Xindi. He was stabbed by a Xindi-Reptilian.

ENT "ZERO HOUR"

Chief Engineer Olson The redshirt trend followed into the *Kelvin* Timeline when this crewman waited too long to pull his chute while on a space jump with Kirk and Sulu to try and disable Nero's orbital drill platform. He was pulled into the drill's beam and killed.

STAR TREK (2009)

THE HONORED DEAD

Redshirts aren't the only ones in danger in the future. The stakes can be so high that sometimes only a brave sacrifice can save the ship, or even the entire Galaxy. Sometimes, the sacrifice is more personal. These are some of the Starfleet heroes who died in the line of duty:

Gary Mitchell A close friend of Captain Kirk's since their time in Starfleet Academy, Mitchell had risked his life for Kirk before their voyage to the galactic barrier. Mitchell gained godlike powers and attempted to kill Kirk, before the captain could stop him.

TOS "WHERE NO MAN HAS GONE BEFORE"

Will Decker When it became clear the V'Ger entity needed a human to merge with to advance its evolution, the first officer of the refit *Enterprise*, Will Decker, volunteered and his former life came to an end.

STAR TREK: THE MOTION PICTURE

Spock Spock sacrificed himself by entering the *Enterprise*'s damaged reactor core to get the engines back online only moments before the Genesis Device destroyed the Mutara Nebula and everything in it.

STAR TREK II: THE WRATH OF KHAN.

Tasha Yar The *Enterprise*-D security chief was callously killed by the powerful being known as Armus during a mission to rescue Counselor Troi.

TNG "SKIN OF EVIL"

Data The crew of the *U.S.S. Enterprise*-E found themselves in battle with Shinzon and the Reman warship, *Scimitar*, shortly after discovering another Soong-type android like Data, called B-4. Saving the *Enterprise* cost Data his life. When Picard spoke of his late friend, he said that the android's quest for humanity "allowed all of us to see what it means to be human."

STAR TREK NEMESIS

Jadzia While the majority of her crew mates were away fighting the first battle of Chin'Toka, Jadzia Dax took command of Deep Space 9. She was killed when she tried to stop Gul Dukat and the Pah-wraith inhabiting his body from imprisoning the Prophets in the wormhole. The Dax symbiont survived and was transferred to Ezri Dax while Worf mourned the loss of the woman he loved.

DS9 "TEARS OF THE PROPHETS"

James T. Kirk The legendary Starfleet captain was presumed killed while saving the *U.S.S. Enterprise* NCC-1701-B during its maiden flight turned rescue mission but he was actually trapped in the dimensional phenomenon known as the Nexus. Captain Picard entered the paradise-like Nexus and convinced Kirk to return to reality and save a star from Dr. Soran's attempt to alter the Nexus's course. Soran caused Kirk to fall to his death, even as his plot failed.

STAR TREK GENERATIONS

Maxwell Forrest In pre-Federation days, Admiral Forrest had to walk a fine line between supporting the nascent Starfleet and following the more experienced Vulcan government. When a terrorist attacked the Earth embassy on Vulcan, Forrest's valor was proved one last time when he sacrificed himself to save Vulcan Ambassador Soval.

ENT "THE FORGE"

Charles "Trip" Tucker The brave *Enterprise* NX-01 chief engineer sacrificed himself to save his captain when the ship was boarded. Tucker rigged a plasma junction to explode and kill the intruders, but he was caught up in the explosion and died from his wounds.

ENT "THESE ARE THE VOYAGES. . ."

Admiral Pike In the *Kelvin* Timeline, Christopher Pike was a mentor to the young Captain Kirk, even managing to help him salvage his career after a disastrous Prime Directive violation. Pike died at the hands of Khan, leaving the enraged Kirk to hunt down his mentor's killer.

STAR TREK INTO DARKNESS

Spock The former *Enterprise* first officer lived a full life in his original timeline before getting caught in the string of events that created the *Kelvin* Timeline. With the destruction of the Planet Vulcan, Spock took on the role of helping his people rebuild their civilization. Ultimately, the character's life was memorialized on film following the passing of his portrayer, Leonard Nimoy.

STAR TREK BEYOND

PERHAPS ONE OF THE BEST THINGS ABOUT FICTION, ESPECIALLY SCIENCE FICTION, IS THAT THE NORMAL RULES DON'T APPLY. IF A CHARACTER DIES, THERE'S NO REASON THEY CAN'T COME BACK . . . ESPECIALLY IN A UNIVERSE THAT DEALS WITH NANOPROBES, VULCAN MYSTICISM, AND GOD-LIKE COSMIC ENTITIES ON A REGULAR BASIS. SOME OF THE *STAR TREK* CHARACTERS THAT "GOT BETTER" INCLUDE:

Kirk The famed Starfleet captain experienced several miraculous resurrections, beginning with the time he was presumed dead when Spock appeared to kill him during the Vulcan marriage challenge. (Dr. McCoy had given the captain a tri-ox compound that simulated death.) Spock later used a "Vulcan death grip" to trick the Romulans into thinking he had killed Kirk. Years later, the captain was ultimately believed to be truly dead after the destruction of the *Enterprise*-B, but he was actually trapped in the bliss of the cosmic phenomenon known as the Nexus for almost a century until his actual death. (Although the captain was resurrected in the non-canon novel series written by William Shatner.) Kirk's imperviousness to death continued in the *Kelvin* Timeline when he died saving the ship from Khan and was revived using the unique properties of the eugenics warlord's blood.

TOS "AMOK TIME"/"THE ENTERPRISE INCIDENT"/ STAR TREK GENERATIONS/STAR TREK INTO DARKNESS

Spock The first officer died in the Prime Timeline while saving the *Enterprise* when Khan launched the Genesis torpedo. He was brought back to life through the Vulcan *fal-tor-pan* ceremony.

STAR TREK II: THE WRATH OF KHAN/ STAR TREK III: THE SEARCH FOR SPOCK

Data The android was effectively deactivated by decapitation, and then reactivated when his five hundred-year-old severed head was reattached. Years later, it was implied that he may have lived on after dying to save the *Enterprise*-E, thanks to an earlier download with his "brother," B-4.

TNG "TIME'S ARROW, PART II"/STAR TREK NEMESIS

McCoy The chief medical officer died at the hands of a jousting knight on the shore leave planet, but the unique factory under the surface of the planet "repaired" him.

TOS "SHORE LEAVE"

Scotty Nomad killed the chief engineer, but it also revived him.

TOS "THE CHANGELING"

Picard The captain phasered his future self to end the time loop the crew was caught in, but the present version of him survived the attack. Picard also died while undergoing heart surgery but got a second chance at life thanks to the omnipotent powers of Q.

TNG "TIME SQUARED"/"TAPESTRY"

Janeway The Doctor thought he lost his captain several times after she seemed to die in a shuttle accident, but she fought back to dislodge an alien presence in her cerebral cortex attempting to make her leave life behind.

VGR "CODA"

Neelix A beam of energy from a protomatter transport killed the Talaxian, who was revived eighteen hours later by Borg nano probes, but this was not the Talaxian's first brush with death. A couple years earlier he and Tuvok ceased to exist as individuals when their bodies and personalities were merged in a transporter accident that created the new lifeform, christened Tuvix, until Janeway destroyed the new being to bring back her crewmen.

VGR "MORTAL COIL"/"TUVIX"

FAMILY MATTERS

EVEN IN THE FUTURE, THE BONDS OF FAMILY CAN SUPPORT AND SOMETIMES BIND. NO MATTER WHAT PLANET A STARFLEET OFFICER COMES FROM, CHANCES ARE THERE IS SOMEONE WAITING FOR THEIR SAFE RETURN, OR READY TO FOLLOW IN THEIR FOOTSTEPS.

The Sisko Family Benjamin Sisko met Jennifer on Gilgo Beach and they married shortly after that. Their son, Jake, was born a year later. Jennifer was tragically killed during the Battle of Wolf 359 when the entire family was aboard the *U.S.S. Saratoga* while Benjamin was stationed there. The loss embittered Sisko for years and he nearly resigned his Starfleet commission. Instead, he and Jake transferred to Deep Space 9, where he eventually found love again with Kasidy Yates. During this time, Ben Sisko learned more about his own parentage and his father's relationship with a woman who had been possessed by a Bajoran Prophet.

DS9 "EMISSARY"/"THE JEM'HADAR"/"IMAGE IN THE SAND"

The Crusher Family When Beverly Crusher accepted a position on the *Enterprise*-D, she was able to bring her son, Wesley, along as it was one of the ships in the fleet with family quarters. This was especially important to the doctor as they were both still mourning the loss of Wesley's father, Jack.

Peter Kirk Captain Kirk's nephew was orphaned when neural parasites attacked the colony on Deneva where he lived with his parents, George and Aurelan Kirk. The *Enterprise* crew found out how to destroy the parasites too late to save the colony, but Kirk managed to save his nephew.

TOS "OPERATION—ANNIHILATE!"

Demora Sulu An assignment aboard the *Enterprise*-B placed the daughter of Hikaru Sulu where her father previously sat: at the helm. She was on board during the ship's maiden voyage, making her a witness to the presumed death of her father's former captain, James T. Kirk.

STAR TREK GENERATIONS

David Marcus For most of his life, the son of Dr. Carol Marcus had no clue that Admiral James T. Kirk was his father. Their relationship was initially strained when they met on the Regula planetoid, but he grew to appreciate his father. David ultimately sacrificed his life to save Saavik from the Klingons who had captured them.

STAR TREK II: THE WRATH OF KHAN/ STAR TREK III: THE SEARCH FOR SPOCK

The Picard Family Captain Jean-Luc Picard came from a proud lineage in France. His father, Maurice, owned a vineyard that his older brother Robert eventually inherited when Jean-Luc decided to join Starfleet. Robert married a woman named Marie and had a son, Rene, who also dreamed of exploring the stars. Tragically, Rene and Robert died in a fire at the family home, just prior to Captain Picard's encounter with the Nexus phenomenon.

TNG "FAMILY"/STAR TREK GENERATIONS

The Soong Lineage The Soong family tree was interspersed with both Human and cybernetic branches. Arik Soong was a geneticist during the Eugenics War and postulated the existence of true cybernetic life-forms. Noonien Soong met and married Juliana O'Donnell and created three functioning Soong-type androids: the primitive B-4, Lore, and Data. When Juliana was fatally injured, Soong transferred her memory into another android body. The new Juliana was unaware she was an android. Soong himself died after mistakenly gifting Lore with an emotion chip he planned for Data. And Data himself took on his father's work by creating his own offspring in the short-lived android Lal.

TNG "DATALORE"/"BROTHERS"/"INHERITANCE"/ STAR TREK NEMESIS/ ENT "THE AUGMENTS"

Ishara Yar Tasha Yar cared for her sister after their parents' death on the brutal and lawless planet Turkana IV. Ishara felt betrayed by her sister for leaving her behind to join Starfleet, and joined the Coalition faction on her home world. Long after Tasha's death, Ishara encountered her sister's crewmates from the *Enterprise*-D and reconciled somewhat with the memory of her sister.

TNG "LEGACY"

The O'Brien Family Miles O'Brien met and married Keiko Ishikawa while they served aboard the *Enterprise*-D. They had a daughter, Molly, while still aboard and before moving to Deep Space 9. After Keiko was injured while pregnant with their son, Kirayoshi, the baby was brought to term using Kira Nerys as a surrogate. After several years together on DS9, the family moved again, for a quieter posting on Earth.

TNG "DATA'S DAY"/
DS9 "THE BEGOTTEN"/"WHAT YOU LEAVE BEHIND"

Lwaxana Troi The wildly eccentric and outrageous mother of Counselor Deanna Troi, Lwaxana was a skilled ambassador for the Federation. Deanna loved her mother, though she was often embarrassed by the flamboyant woman's antics whenever she visited. But Lwaxana had depths she rarely showed, and Deanna was instrumental in helping her mother accept the death of her eldest daughter, Kestra.

TNG "DARK PAGE"

Sarek/Amanda Spock's parents made an unusual coupling, the stoic Vulcan ambassador and the graceful, yet emotional Human teacher. Still, they were devoted to each other, and he claimed he married her because at the time, "it seemed like the logical thing to do." Vulcan lifespans are longer than Human, and after Amanda died, Sarek took another Human wife named Perrin. Though Sarek and Spock were estranged, mind-melds with Captian Picard allowed Spock a better understanding of his father after Sarek's death.

TOS "JOURNEY TO BABEL"/
TNG "SAREK"

Henry Archer Colleague of Zefram Cochrane and father to *Enterprise* NX-01 Captain Jonathan Archer, Henry was the developer of the first warp 5-capable engine. Due to the Vulcan opposition to the Warp 5 program, Henry, who suffered from the debilitating Clarke's Disease, never saw his goal completed.

ENT "BROKEN BOW"

Q Family Family units are hard to define with cosmic entities such as the Q. Nevertheless, at the suggestion of Captain Janeway, the male and female Q attempted to end their continuum's civil war by mating. The offspring caused trouble for the parents, but another visit to *Voyager* helped Q learn how to discipline his omnipotent son.

VGR "THE Q AND THE GREY"/Q2"

LOVE, STARFLEET STYLE

RELATIONSHIPS IN SPACE CAN QUITE LITERALLY BE STAR-CROSSED. HOWEVER, THE HUMAN (AND ALIEN) NEED FOR LOVE AND COMPANIONSHIP ALWAYS SEEMS TO FIND A WAY. WHETHER SEPARATED BY LIGHT-YEARS OF DISTANCE OR TRAPPED ON THE SAME SHIP FOR MONTHS, THESE EPIC LOVE STORIES SHOW THAT, MORE OFTEN THAN NOT, LOVE WILL FIND A WAY.

Chapel/Spock After her first love, Dr. Roger Korby, died, Nurse Christine Chapel's affections turned to the stoic Mr. Spock. While there was never hope for the relationship with the logical Vulcan, she often reached out to him with kind gestures like making plomeek soup. When she became a doctor and saw Spock for the first time in years during the V'Ger mission, she was pleased to reconnect with him, but the old infatuation had cooled.

TOS "AMOK TIME"

Kira/Odo Galaxy-crossed lovers, Odo had been in love with Kira for years but never told her. An alternate version of himself from another timeline convinced him to let her know how he felt. They became lovers, but after the Dominion war, Odo felt he had no choice but to return to his people and ensure they would keep the peace. He reluctantly left Kira, who now commanded Deep Space 9.

DS9 "HEART OF STONE"/"WHAT YOU LEAVE BEHIND"

Worf/Troi After a *bat'leth* tournament, Worf found himself quantum shifting between parallel universes. In one of these, he and Deanna Troi were married. The experience led him to pursue a relationship with the counselor. They dated for a period of time, but ultimately the relationship faded away like a quantum reality.

TNG "PARALLELS"

Data/Yar More of a fling than a relationship, when members of the crew were under the intoxicating effects of the Psi 2000 virus, Lieutenant Yar questioned whether Data was "fully functional." He proved that he was, and the incident caused some angry embarrassment for Yar afterward, but also resulted in a close bond that the android cherished beyond her death.

TNG "THE NAKED NOW"

Riker/Troi When the young Will Riker was stationed on Betazed, he fell in love with Deanna Troi. They became *Imzadi*, a Betazoid word meaning "beloved," with lifelong connotations. For Riker, his Starfleet career came first and he left without seeing her again, certain that he would not be able to say good-bye. Years later, they were assigned to the *Enterprise*-D and they both had to reexamine their feelings. Their mission to the Ba'ku planet solidified their love for each other, and the two married when Riker was assigned his own command.

TNG "HAVEN"/*STAR TREK: INSURRECTION*/
STAR TREK NEMESIS

Kirk/Carol Marcus The relationship between James Kirk and Carol Marcus was brief but produced their son, David. Carol never told David who his father was, as she wanted to keep him with her and not running around the Galaxy like his father. When they reunited on the Regula planetoid, Carol was pleased to see Kirk, but there was no sign she wanted to revive the relationship.

STAR TREK II: THE WRATH OF KHAN

Scotty/Uhura After working together for so many years, Scotty's and Uhura's mutual admiration had deepened. Their intimate exchange on the bridge of the *U.S.S. Enterprise*-A hinted at more, but whether even their close colleagues knew of the relationship is uncertain.

STAR TREK V: THE FINAL FRONTIER

Sisko/Yates Jake Sisko introduced his father to Kasidy, the captain of the freighter ship *Xhosa*. The two bonded over a passion for baseball and fell in love. They eventually married and she became pregnant soon before the end of the Dominion war. When Sisko joined the Prophets he appeared to her to say he would be back, "maybe in a year, maybe yesterday."

DS9 "FOR THE CAUSE"/"TIL DEATH DO US PART"/
"WHAT YOU LEAVE BEHIND"

Worf/Dax The Dax symbiont had previous deep ties with Klingon culture, so it was not surprising the Jadzia host would find Worf attractive. The two began a relationship that culminated in a traditional Klingon wedding on Deep Space 9. Sadly, Jadzia was killed soon after by a Pah-wraith inhabiting Gul Dukat. The new host, Ezri, cared for Worf, but eventually found love with Dr. Bashir.

DS9 "YOU ARE CORDIALLY INVITED . . ."/
"WHAT YOU LEAVE BEHIND"

Chakotay/Seven of Nine After years together in the Delta Quadrant, Chakotay and the former Borg Seven of Nine found themselves romantically attracted to one another. Seven felt strongly enough about attempting to pursue the relationship to have the Doctor disable Borg fail-safes that were inhibiting her emotions.

VGR "ENDGAME"

O'Brien/Keiko Data introduced Miles and Keiko to each other while they served aboard the *Enterprise*-D, and the android stood in as "father of the bride" in their wedding. When Chief O'Brien transferred to DS9, Keiko and their daughter, Molly, accompanied him, although for Keiko, the station never felt like home. After the Dominion War, he accepted a job on Earth and the family moved again.

TNG "DATA'S DAY"/DS9 "WHAT YOU LEAVE BEHIND"

Torres/Paris The half Klingon B'Elanna Torres spent her life keeping people at arm's length, and she was no different when Tom Paris showed interest in a relationship. On the Klingon Day of Honor, when she believed she was about to die, she confessed that she did love him. The two eloped and she became pregnant, giving birth just as *Voyager* returned home to the Alpha Quadrant.

VGR "DAY OF HONOR"/"ENDGAME"

T'Pol/Tripp What started as therapeutic Vulcan neuropressure sessions led T'Pol and Tripp to face their attraction and they ended up becoming intimate. However, the relationship never got off the ground due to factors beyond their control. The xenophobic group Terra Prime stole their DNA and created their "daughter," Elizabeth, to foster fear between Humans and aliens. The baby died due to flaws in the genetic process, but T'Pol and Tripp remained close until his death.

ENT "THE XINDI"/ "HARBINGER"/"HOME"

Spock/Uhura In the *Kelvin* Timeline, Spock and Uhura began a relationship while she was a cadet. She understood his focus on logic, though they did fight over what she saw as needless risks. The relationship ended before the *Enterprise*'s mission to Starbase Yorktown, though there were indications that they both still had feelings for each other.

STAR TREK (2009)/
STAR TREK INTO DARKNESS/
STAR TREK BEYOND

LIST #17 GENERATION GAP

Born in the throes of the 1960s, when the generation gap was never more apparent, the youth generation adopted the hopeful vision of the future that *Star Trek* represented. Onscreen, however, the youth voice was often not as representative as one might think. In fact, Captain Picard once noted there was no place for children on a starship. Nevertheless, the crews often ran into many and even ended up taking children under their wings.

Miri Orphaned and long-lived children from an experiment gone wrong, Miri and the other preteen children of her planet were in danger of a disease the "grups" (grown-ups) had caused.

TOS "MIRI"

Icheb, Mezoti, Azan, and Rebi After Icheb's father used him as the delivery system for a Borg-killing virus, Icheb and three other assimilated children were all that survived aboard a Borg cube. The children created their own mini collective until they were rescued and came to live aboard the *U.S.S. Voyager*.

VGR "COLLECTIVE"

Starnes Exploration Party The noncorporeal entity known as the Gorgan caused the adults in the exploratory party to commit suicide. Appearing to the children as a "Friendly Angel," the creature managed to use them to control the minds of the *Enterprise* crew until Kirk made the children face their grief over their parents, sending the Gorgan to oblivion.

TOS "AND THE CHILDREN SHALL LEAD"

Wesley Crusher Teenage genius Wesley was the son of Dr. Beverly and Jack Crusher. While Captain Picard was initially irritated with Wesley's presence on the bridge, as the teen matured, he became a valuable crew member and earned Picard's respect.

TNG "ENCOUNTER AT FARPOINT" / "FINAL MISSION"

Alexander After the death of his mother, K'Ehlyr, Alexander went to live with his grandparents on Earth before joining Worf on the *Enterprise*-D. Though Worf was unprepared to be a single parent, he and Alexander managed to become a family.

TNG "REUNION"/"NEW GROUND" / DS9 "SONS AND DAUGHTERS"

Charlie X An orphan raised by godlike aliens, Charlie tried to fit in aboard the *Enterprise*, but he was unable to deal with the frustration of being a normal teenage male. The powerful Thasians returned him to their care after Charlie's powers wreaked havoc on the crew.

TOS "CHARLIE X"

Molly & Kirayoshi O'Brien Molly was born aboard the *Enterprise*-D and came to Deep Space 9 with her parents, after which Kirayoshi was born on a runabout.

TNG "DISASTER"/DS9 "IF WISHES WERE HORSES" / "WHAT YOU LEAVE BEHIND"

Jake Sisko Jake accompanied his father to Deep Space 9 after the death of his mother. He befriended Nog and their association inspired the Ferengi to be the first of his race to join Starfleet. Jake took a different path as a novelist and war correspondent for the Federation News Service.

DS9 "EMISSARY"/"CALL TO ARMS" / "YOU ARE CORDIALLY INVITED"

Nog At first, Rom's son seemed to be a typical Ferengi, always looking for the profit in any situation. Eventually inspired by Captain Sisko and other Starfleet personnel aboard the station, Nog applied to Starfleet Academy and was accepted as the first Ferengi in Starfleet.

DS9 "PROGRESS"/"IT'S ONLY A PAPER MOON"

Naomi Wildman The half Ktarian Naomi was the first child born on the *U.S.S. Voyager* while it was lost in the Delta Quadrant. Her Ktarian genes made her age more quickly than full Humans. The responsible child asked Captain Janeway if she could become her "bridge assistant," and was granted that request. Neelix served as her godfather.

VGR "DEADLOCK"/"ONCE UPON A TIME"

ENGAGE!

As captain of the *U.S.S. Enterprise*-D, Jean-Luc Picard was a more reserved and private person than captains who had come before him. He nevertheless valued romance and fell in love several times during his tenure aboard the *Enterprise*. Though his command to set the ship in motion ("Engage!") was often heard on the bridge, Picard never set his romantic life in motion in quite the same way.

Jenice Manheim Almost twenty years before Picard took command of the *Enterprise*-D, he fell in love with Jenice while in Paris. They agreed to meet at the Cafe des Artistes before he shipped out on assignment, but Picard failed to show because he was afraid he would lose himself in the relationship. The pair reconnected when the *Enterprise* traveled to Pegos Minor to help Jenice's husband, and they were able to share a proper good-bye.

TNG "WE'LL ALWAYS HAVE PARIS"

Beverly Crusher The relationship between the captain and chief medical officer of the *Enterprise*-D was complicated by the fact that Crusher's husband, Jack, died while under Picard's command on the *U.S.S. Stargazer*. Crusher's and Picard's feelings sometimes surfaced during their time together, however, they maintained a deep and intimate friendship without letting those feelings develop. In the anti-time future that Q showed Picard, he and Beverly did in fact marry, then later divorce.

TNG "ENCOUNTER AT FARPOINT"/"ALL GOOD THINGS . . ."

Vash The beautiful archaeologist and profiteer first encountered Picard while he was on holiday on Risa. Their mutual love for artifacts turned into a romantic encounter. They parted ways because her amoral lifestyle was not compatible with that of a respected starship captain, but met again when Q brought them together. The reunion rekindled their feelings, but she opted to leave him again to travel with the more like-minded Q.

TNG "CAPTAIN'S HOLIDAY"/"QPID"

Nella Daren A love of music began the bond between the brash head of the Stellar Sciences department and Captain Picard. But when their relationship compromised his command decisions, Daren transferred off the ship rather than having either of them give up their careers.

TNG "LESSONS"

Guinan One of the great mysteries of the universe is the relationship between Guinan and Captain Picard that the bartender considered "beyond friendship . . . beyond family."

TNG "THE BEST OF BOTH WORLDS, PART II"

Kamala An accidental telepathic bonding created the perfect relationship for Picard, but his own sense of duty demanded that they remain apart.

TNG "THE PERFECT MATE"

Eline While not technically Picard's love, Eline shared a lifetime of wedded bliss with the captain when a probe implanted memories of a man named Kamin from the long-forgotten planet of Ressik.

TNG "THE INNER LIGHT"

Anij The Ba'ku woman mistrusted Picard at first, but they fell in love as they worked to save her people from the Son'a. After the Son'a were defeated, Picard told her he had 318 days of shore leave coming and he intended to use them.

STAR TREK: INSURRECTION

Miranda Vigo Years after Picard had a brief affair with the botanist, DaiMon Bok used that relationship to briefly trick the captain into believing that he had a son.

TNG "BLOODLINES"

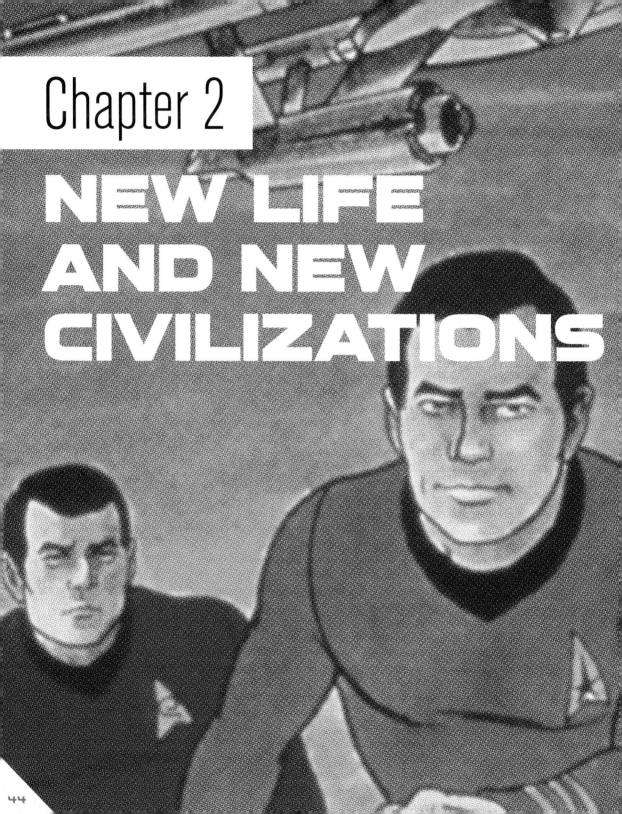

Chapter 2
NEW LIFE AND NEW CIVILIZATIONS

FIRST CONTACT

As the Starfleet crews trekked farther out into unknown territory, they encountered truly new species for the first time. Each encounter brought the potential to expand the Federation or destroy it, so captains had strict protocols for dealing with alien species for the first time, depending on the technology level of the culture. These are just a few of the more notable first contacts witnessed in the series.

Talosians First contact made by Captain Christopher Pike of the *U.S.S. Enterprise*, who returned to live among them when his body was destroyed in an accident.

TOS "THE MENAGERIE"

Horta First contact made by Captain James T. Kirk and Mr. Spock of the *U.S.S. Enterprise*.

TOS "THE DEVIL IN THE DARK"

Gorn First contact made by Captain James T. Kirk of the *U.S.S. Enterprise*.

TOS "ARENA"

Klingons First contact by an Earth farmer and crew of *Enterprise* NX-01 on what became their maiden voyage. The *Enterprise* crew would go on to make first Human contact with many alien races that would eventually become allies, including the founding members of the Federation in the Andorians and Tellarites.

ENT "BROKEN BOW"/"THE ANDORIAN INCIDENT"/"BOUNTY"

Ferengi First contact made by the crew of the *U.S.S. Enterprise*-D. (Although, technically speaking, a time-travel mishap led to unofficial first contact with members of the United States military on Earth in 1947.)

TNG "THE LAST OUTPOST"/DS9 "LITTLE GREEN MEN"

Borg First contact made by the crew of the *U.S.S. Enterprise*-D, thanks to the "help" of Q.

TNG "Q WHO"

Prophets First contact made by Benjamin Sisko, who was newly assigned to Deep Space 9 (decades after his mother was possessed by a member of the noncorporeal race).

DS9 "EMISSARY"

Changelings First contact with an individual Changeling (Odo) made by Dr. Mora Pol of the Bajoran Institute for Science. First contact with the race of Founders made by Odo.

DS9 "THE SEARCH"

Kazon First contact made by the crew of the *U.S.S. Voyager*.

VGR "CARETAKER"

Hirogen First contact made by the crew of the *U.S.S. Voyager*.

VGR "MESSAGE IN A BOTTLE"

Vulcans First official contact by Zefram Cochrane, with an assist from the time-traveling crew of the *U.S.S. Enterprise*-E. (Unofficial first contact occurred over a century earlier when a Vulcan crew was stranded on Earth.)

STAR TREK: FIRST CONTACT/
ENT "CARBON CREEK"

USEFUL KLINGON PHRASES

THE KLINGON LANGUAGE WAS REFERENCED IN THE ORIGINAL SERIES BUT NEVER HEARD UNTIL *STAR TREK: THE MOTION PICTURE*. IRONICALLY, JAMES DOOHAN—WHOSE CHARACTER WOULD LATER SAY, "READING KLINGON; THAT'S HARD!" IN *STAR TREK IV: THE VOYAGE HOME*—HELPED CREATE THE LANGUAGE WITH THE FILM'S ASSOCIATE PRODUCER AND A UCLA DIALECT EXPERT. LINGUIST MARC OKRAND EXPANDED THE LANGUAGE FOR THE SECOND FILM AND WROTE *THE KLINGON DICTIONARY*.

When visiting Qo'noS there are some words and phrases everyone should know.

gik'tal "to the death" (implying combat)

he'ymar "energize" (to activate transporters)

Qapla' "Success!"

par'Mach "love" (but a fairly muscle-pulling, bruise-causing form of love)

petaQ an insult (sometimes combined as "filthy" and "traitorous," implying petaQs are beneath contempt)

Sto-Vo-Kor the Klingon equivalent of "heaven"

Maj ram "Good night"

Heghlu'meH QaQ jajvam "It is a good day to die" (Klingon battle cry)

qaStaHvIS wa' ram loSSaD Hugh SIjlaH qetbogh loD
"Four thousand throats may be cut in one night by a running man" (Klingon proverb)

Jaj vIghaj "Own the day" (Klingon proverb)

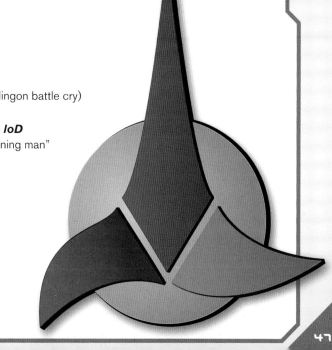

AN ALIEN'S BEST FRIEND

SOME ALIENS IN THE QUADRANT HAVE SLIGHTLY DIFFERENT IDEAS ABOUT WHAT MAKES A GOOD PET.

Tribbles Furry, calming, and born pregnant, tribbles are some of the most adorable pets in the Alpha Quadrant—unless you're a Klingon. The little fur balls procreate at an alarming rate, multiplying exponentially. On their home world, reptilian predators keep the population in check, and Dr. McCoy eventually discovered that neoethylene could slow their metabolic rate, making them safer as pets.

TOS "THE TROUBLE WITH TRIBBLES"/
TAS "MORE TRIBBLES, MORE TROUBLES"/
DS9 "TRIALS AND TRIBBLE-ATIONS"

Spot During his fourth year serving aboard the *Enterprise*-D, Data acquired the cat he named Spot. Data cared deeply for his pet, composing a poem in iambic septameter called "Ode to Spot." The cat helped save the crew when Data discovered that her newborn kittens were unaffected by Barclay's Protomophosis Syndrome and surmised amniotic fluid could help reverse the effects. Spot survived the crash of the *Enterprise*-D and joined the crew aboard the *Enterprise*-E. (Somewhere along the way, Spot performed the miraculous feat of changing both breed and gender.)

TNG "DATA'S DAY"/"GENESIS"/
STAR TREK GENERATIONS

Sehlat When Doctor McCoy learned Spock once had a teddy bear, he tried to tease the Vulcan. He gave up on the jokes upon finding out Vulcan sehlats are alive and have six-inch fangs. Spock's sehlat saved his life, but was poisoned by another animal, and the young Spock had to make the logical decision to let his pet, I-Chaya, die with dignity. T'Pol, science officer on the *Enterprise* NX-01, also owned a sehlat in her youth.

TOS "JOURNEY TO BABEL"/
TAS "YESTERYEAR"/ENT "THE FORGE"

Christina Before Chief O'Brien moved to Deep Space 9, he owned a pet Lycosa tarantula he named Christina. O'Brien overcame his fear of spiders when he had to repair a damaged emitter array and climbed past twenty Talarian hook spiders. He almost stepped on Christina when he first encountered her, and he kept her to celebrate his triumph over his arachnophobia. It's not known if Christina moved to Deep Space 9, or had trouble with O'Brien's later pet cat, Chester.

TNG "REALM OF FEAR"

Targ Vicious, furry, and boar-like in appearance, these wild animals are often kept by Klingons as pets. Lieutenant Worf had one as a child. High frequency tones will disperse herds of wild *targs*, and Klingon ground assault vehicles use these devices to prevent collisions. Heart of *targ* is a popular dish and Klingons even use the tallow of the animals' shoulders to make candles.

TNG "WHERE NO ONE HAS GONE BEFORE"/
DS9 "YOU ARE CORDIALLY INVITED . . ."

"Livingston" Captain Picard's traveling companion was a lionfish that resided in a tank in his ready room during his command of the *Enterprise*-D. Although the fish was never named onscreen, the production crew christened him "Livingston" in honor of producer-director David Livingston.

TNG "CHAIN OF COMMAND"

Isis The companion to advanced humanoid Gary Seven was a black cat who communicated with Seven telepathically. She could also take human form, but Seven's secretary, Roberta Lincoln, was the only one who appeared to notice this when Spock and Kirk encountered them in 1968.

TOS "ASSIGNMENT: EARTH"

Pyrithian bat Dr. Phlox's pet bat never had a name, but the physician cared for it dutifully. The bat sometimes escaped from its cage, and would even come to Lieutenant Hoshi when called. The bat enjoyed a variety of foods including Vulcan sandworms, moth larvae, and snow beetles.

ENT "A NIGHT IN SICKBAY"

Porthos Captain Jonathan Archer's faithful companion was a beagle named after one of the Three Musketeers. Archer had the dog since Porthos was only six weeks old. While he didn't do any tricks, he did have an unrivaled love of cheese. In the mirror universe, Porthos had a different temperament and breed: he was a Rottweiler that disliked strangers.

ENT "A NIGHT IN SICKBAY"/
"IN A MIRROR, DARKLY"

NOW YOU SEE ME . . . NOW YOU DON'T

THE GALAXY IS A BIG PLACE, AND THE VARIETY OF LIFE IS NEARLY INFINITE. WHILE HUMANOID FORMS SEEM TO POP UP EVERYWHERE, OBEYING HODGKINS'S LAW OF PARALLEL PLANET DEVELOPMENT, THERE ARE PLENTY OF LIFEFORMS THAT ARE COMPLETELY ALIEN. ONE SUCH FORM IS THE NONCORPOREAL, WHICH MEANS THE ENTITY HAS NO PHYSICAL BODY, AND IS USUALLY COMPOSED OF ENERGY OR EVEN PURE MIND. OFTEN THESE BEINGS HAVE EXTRAORDINARY POWERS, AND CAN EVEN TAKE OVER A HUMANOID BODY TEMPORARILY.

Thasians The Thasians had long since evolved to beings of pure mental energy by the time young Charlie Evans's transport ship crashed on their planet. They adopted the three-year-old orphan, whom they gifted with incredible telekinetic powers.

TOS "CHARLIE X"

Redjac The energy-based entity Redjac was a murderer that fed on the emotion of fear. Known as Jack the Ripper in London and as Kesla on Deneb II, the killer traveled from planet to planet in search of victims until it encountered the *Enterprise* crew on Argelius II.

TOS "WOLF IN THE FOLD"

Zalkonian A race on the verge of evolving into a non-corporeal form, any Zalkonians who showed signs of mutating into the next stage were feared and put to death. One, known as John Doe to the *Enterprise*-D crew, managed to escape his government and became the first of his kind to achieve a non-corporeal state.

TNG "TRANSFIGURATIONS"

Dikironium cloud creature Dikironium was a rare gas that composed the substance of the interstellar cloud creature that killed many of the *U.S.S. Farragut*'s crew. The entity was vampiric, feeding off red blood cells and emitting a distinct sickly sweet odor. It also had the ability be out of sync with time, effectively being two places at once.

TOS "OBSESSION"

Kes The young Ocampan believed that her people once had tremendous mental powers. When she met Tania and Suspiria, she found she also had untapped abilities. She ultimately transformed into a non-corporeal being and used her powers to help *Voyager* one last time, by pushing the starship almost ten thousand light-years closer to home.

VGR "THE GIFT"

Douwd The immortal race of energy beings known as the Douwd had immense power and could assume almost any form. When the one who destroyed the entire Husnock race felt regret over his act, he isolated himself as penance with the illusion of his wife.

TNG "THE SURVIVORS"

Companion When the Human inventor of warp drive, Zefram Cochrane, was lost in space and near death, the cloudlike entity known as the Companion rescued and healed him, effectively making him immortal.

TOS "METAMORPHOSIS"

Onaya A deadly muse, Onaya fed off the creativity produced by the humanoid brain. She would stimulate the chemicals involved in the process of those she fed off, and increase that creativity, at the cost of years off the creator's life.

DS9 "THE MUSE"

Komar Living in a dark matter nebula within the Delta Quadrant, the Komar were composed of trianic energy. They fed off of the neural energy of other beings and attacked the crew of the *U.S.S. Voyager* as they traveled through the nebula.

VGR "CATHEXIS"

Medusans A non-corporeal race known for the beauty of their minds, the Medusans had a visible appearance that was so hideous, a Human looking at one would instantly be driven mad.

TOS "IS THERE IN TRUTH NO BEAUTY?"

Gorgan The entity known as the Gorgan appeared to the children of a scientific expedition on Triacus. After causing the adults to commit suicide, the Gorgan tried to use the children to hijack the *Enterprise*.

TOS "AND THE CHILDREN SHALL LEAD"

DON'T JUDGE A
BOOK BY ITS COVER

In the same way the chameleon evolved on Earth to blend in with its environment, many alien races developed similar abilities. Some have the power to not only blend in, but to change their shape completely and assume a different form. Caution (and blood screenings) are advisable when dealing with these creatures.

M-113 Creature Last of its kind, the creature was a "salt vampire" that could extract the mineral directly from the blood cells of its victims. It could assume almost any humanoid shape, and hypnotize Humans at close range.

TOS "THE MAN TRAP"

Antosians/Garth of Izar The inhabitants of Antos IV helped repair the wounded body of Starfleet captain Garth of Izar by teaching him their technique of cellular metamorphosis, not realizing an accident had driven him insane. He destroyed their planet and was committed to the insane asylum on Elba II where he used his metamorphic powers to change shape and take over the asylum for a time.

TOS "WHOM GODS DESTROY"

Sylvia/Korob These alien beings came from outside the Galaxy. They could take human form and perform other amazing feats through the use of their transmuter, a device that uses mental impulses to shape the physical world.

TOS "CATSPAW"

Devidians The Devidians not only have the power to change shape, but can also travel through time, which allowed a pair of them to feed off Human neural energy and use their abilities to kill Humans in nineteenth-century San Francisco.

TNG "TIME'S ARROW"

Dee'Ahn's species A pair of shape-shifting humanoids appeared as beautiful women to lure Tucker and Reed into an ambush on Risa. The two women morphed into their true shapes: spiny, pointed-eared males that attacked Reed and Tucker.

ENT "TWO DAYS AND TWO NIGHTS"

Allasomorphs Natives of Daled IV and its moons are allasomorphs, able to change their molecular structure into other lifeforms.

TNG "THE DAUPHIN"

Chameloids Marta, a Chameloid prisoner on the Klingon prison planet Rura Penthe, was offered a pardon if she helped set up the murder of Kirk and McCoy in an attempted escape.

STAR TREK VI: THE UNDISCOVERED COUNTRY

Suliban Genetic enhancements gave some Suliban levels of shapeshifting ability, from simple camouflage like an Earth chameleon, to humanoid mimicry. Silik, an agent in the Temporal Cold War, encountered the *Enterprise* NX-01 crew several times and even impersonated Commander Tucker on one occasion.

ENT "BROKEN BOW"/"SHOCKWAVE"/"STORM FRONT"

Founders The Changelings native to the Delta Quadrant originally attempted to live among the "solids," which is their term for non-shapeshifters. The Founders' true forms are liquid, and they have to revert to that state every twenty-four hours. If part of a Changeling is removed from the main body mass, it reverts to liquid, making blood screenings a way to verify who is a Changeling or solid.

DS9 "THE SEARCH"/"HOMEFRONT"

Silver Blood The liquid inhabitants of an inhospitable Class-Y planet in the Delta Quadrant were comprised of a material known as silver blood that was biomimetic, and could duplicate any biological or technological item it touched. It became sentient for the first time when it came into physical contact with members of *Voyager*'s crew, and duplicated them and the ship.

VGR "DEMON"/"COURSE: OBLIVION"

AN INTERGALACTIC MENU

POPULAR FOOD FROM THE FOUR BASIC QUADRANTS . . .

Meatloaf TOS "Charlie X"

Gumbo DS9 "Image in the Sand"

Plomeek **soup** TOS "Amok Time"/ENT "Unexpected"

Rokeg **blood pie** TNG "A Matter of Honor"/"Family"

Heart of **targ** TNG "A Matter of Honor"/VGR "Day of Honor"

Gagh TNG "A Matter of Honor"/"Unification"

Yamok **sauce** DS9 "By Inferno's Light"

Tube grubs DS9 "Ferengi Love Songs"

Kaferian apples TOS "Where No Man Has Gone Before"

Uttaberry crepe TNG "Ménage à Troi"/"Dark Page"

Jumja **stick** DS9 "In the Hands of the Prophets"

Chocolate TNG "The Game"

Leola root VGR "State of Flux"

Nutri-pak ENT "Horizon"

No matter where one roams in the Galaxy, at the end of the day it's nice to kick back with a cocktail or enjoy a beer with some friends . . . or perhaps curling up with a cup of tea and a good book is more one's style. Either way, the *Star Trek* galaxy has numerous beverage options to fit any mood.

Saurian Brandy	TOS "The Man Trap"/TNG "Bloodlines"/ DS9 "Emissary"
Romulan Ale	*Star Trek II: The Wrath of Khan*/ DS9 "Inter Arma Enim Silent Leges"
Andorian Ale	ENT "Cease Fire"/ "Babel One"
Tranya	TOS "The Corbomite Maneuver"/ DS9 "Facets"
Synthehol	TNG "Relics"
Bloodwine	VGR "The Killing Game"/ DS9 "Apocalypse Rising"
Aldebaran Whiskey	TNG "Relics"
Prune Juice (A warrior's drink)	TNG "Yesterday's Enterprise"/ DS9 "The Way of the Warrior"
Earl Grey Tea (Served hot)	TNG "Contagion"
Coffee	DS9 "Whispers"/"Duet"/VGR "Hunters"
Antarian Cider	VGR "Shattered"
Bajoran Spring Wine	DS9 "Ferengi Love Songs"/"Return to Grace"
Samarian Sunset	TNG "Conundrum"
Slusho	*Star Trek* (2009)

CREATING NEW ALIEN RACES WEEK AFTER WEEK CAN BE A CHALLENGE, ESPECIALLY ON THE PRODUCTION BUDGET. THROUGHOUT THE DECADES, THE *STAR TREK* STAFF HAS MANAGED TO MAKE HUMAN ACTORS LOOK EXTREMELY ALIEN WITH ONLY MAKEUP, PROSTHETICS, AND WARDROBE. IN RECENT YEARS, COMPUTER-GENERATED EFFECTS HAVE ENHANCED THE LOOK OF SOME MORE UNIQUE ALIENS, BUT NOTHING CAN COMPARE TO THE MOST MEMORABLE PHYSICAL MAKEUP EFFECTS THAT HAVE SET THE STANDARD FOR THE *STAR TREK* ALIEN AESTHETIC.

Vulcan The simple but effective ears-and-eyebrows combination creates an iconic look that has become synonymous with the franchise.

Klingon The Klingon look on The Original Series was little more than eyebrows and dark face makeup. Once the films began, with their larger budgets, the Klingon look became more elaborate with ridged foreheads. More recently, the Klingon look has evolved with the *Kelvin* Timeline films and *Star Trek: Discovery*.

Romulan The Original Series Romulans also underwent a transition once they appeared in *The Next Generation*. The twenty-fourth-century Romulans have a pronounced V-shape to their forehead.

Andorian Blue skin and antennae make these aliens stand head and shoulders above the others. CGI effects have been used to animate their atennae in the later series.

Tellarite The distinctive snout of these TOS aliens made them a memorable alien makeup design. Though they appeared in The Animated Series and a pair of films, it wasn't until *Enterprise* that these founding members of the Federation saw their most dramatic redesign, taking their look to the next level.

Talosian Enlarged heads aren't the only illusions these aliens projected; male voices were dubbed coming out of these female guest actors on The Original Series.

Cheron The racism of their planet was metaphorically embodied in the half-black and half-white skin of these TOS aliens.

Orion The green full-body paint arouses envy in women and lust in men.

Borg Part-makeup and part-prop, the cybernetic Borg skin becomes a deathly white once assimilated, no matter the race or species. Tubes and prosthetic or electrical gadgets complete the look.

Ferengi Their four-lobed brains no doubt account for the enlarged cranium appliance used for their heads. The huge ears connect over the eyebrows. The process to apply originally took four hours, but after time, the makeup staff got it down to two hours.

Trill Hosts of the Trill symbionts have a distinctive spotted pattern running down the sides of their faces and the lengths of their bodies.

Bajoran The ridges at the top of the nose create an immediately recognizable look for these aliens.

Cardassian Actors playing the reptilian Cardassians spent a lot of time in the makeup chair. Gray skin and scales, prosthetic neck ridges, and the spoon-like indentation in the forehead took several hours.

Vidiian A virus known as the Phage laid waste to this once-thriving Delta Quadrant society. To visualize this horrific disease, the makeup department used a layered effect to the makeup applications to give the effect that their bodies were literally decomposing.

Species 8472 The *Voyager* crew may never have learned the names of these aliens that reside in fluidic space, but Species 8472 left an indelible mark on the franchise as the first completely computer-generated characters in the franchise.

THE RECREATION ROOM

Even with the thrills and adventure of exploring strange new worlds, a starship crew needs some downtime because the captain won't always allow a quick trip to Risa. Federation starships have recreation rooms available for the crew to gather to play games or sports, while alien species also have some unique ways to blow off steam.

Dabo Similar to an Earth roulette wheel, the dabo table is attended by beautiful dabo girls, whose main function is to distract players into losing their bets.

DS9 "THE ABANDONED"

Fizzbin Kirk made up the perplexing game of fizzbin to distract his captors on Sigma Iotia II. Players are dealt six cards, except the player on the dealer's right, who gets seven. The second card is turned up, except on Tuesdays, and two jacks make a half fizzbin. Don't bother trying to get a royal fizzbin as the odds are astronomical.

TOS "A PIECE OF THE ACTION"

Bat'leth competition A Klingon tournament in which competitors are often severely injured. Worf won Champion Standing in his own reality, but in a parallel universe placed ninth when the judges did not rule against his opponent's illegal T'Gha maneuver.

TNG "PARALLELS"

Parrises squares Four people, armed with ion mallets, make up a pair of teams for a parrises squares match. Though the uniforms are padded, many experience injuries during the rough game.

TNG "11001001"

Hoverball An active game played with an antigravity ball. Lieutenant B'Elanna Torres was a fierce competitor in the sport, even to the point of once finishing a tournament on a broken ankle.

VGR "REMEMBER"

Dom-jot A game much like billiards—though the table is oddly shaped—dom-jot was Jake Sisko's and Nog's favorite game.

DS9 "LITTLE GREEN MEN"

Strategema The holographic strategy game is played by hooking electronic controllers to the fingers and attempting to change the color of the holographic panels. Data defeated Kolrami, a Zakdorn third-level grand master, after theorizing that playing to stalemate would force Kolrami to concede.

TNG "PEAK PERFORMANCE"

Poker The standard Earth game went with mankind into the stars. The bridge officers of the *U.S.S. Enterprise*-D had a weekly game, usually playing five-card stud.

TNG "CAUSE AND EFFECT"

Three-dimensional chess A favorite of captains, first officers, and even genetically enhanced children. This variant of Earth chess is more complicated, with popular moves like the Kriskov Gambit and El-Mitra Exchange.

TOS "CHARLIE X"/TNG "CONUNDRUM"

Ktarian game An addictive game that rewarded the pleasure center of the brain as someone played, increasing dependence on the game. The game nearly took over the entire crew of the *Enterprise*-D, until visiting cadet Wesley Crusher managed to help Data free the crew.

TNG "THE GAME"

Kal-toh Tuvok claimed the Vulcan strategy game was as to chess as chess was to tic-tac-toe. The game, in which rods are used to create a perfect sphere, symbolizes finding order among chaos. Single or multiple people can play.

VGR "ALTER EGO"

61

FOR CENTURIES, MARTIAL ARTS DEVELOPED ON EARTH NOT ONLY AS SELF-DEFENSE BUT AS A METHOD OF STRENGTHENING BOTH MIND AND BODY. FOR STARFLEET PERSONNEL, THE MARTIAL ARTS PROVIDED A NONLETHAL METHOD OF DEFENSE WHEN HUMANS BEGAN TO EXPLORE DEEP-SPACE. OF COURSE, MANY OTHER CULTURES WERE DEVELOPING SIMILAR ARTS, WHICH WERE GLIMPSED THROUGHOUT THE SERIES.

Tsunkatse This form of fighting to the death is a spectator sport in the Delta Quadrant. Opponents battle each other wearing polaron disruptors on their hands and feet that cause bioplasmic charges if they hit sensors on an opponent's body.

VGR "TSUNKATSE"

Anbo-jyutsu The ultimate expression of martial arts in the twenty-fourth century—according to Commander Riker's father, Kyle—has competitors wearing armor while blindfolded by a visor. A staff with a proximity sensor and rounded cushion on opposite ends is used to attack an opponent.

TNG "THE ICARUS FACTOR"

Tal-shaya This ancient Vulcan technique is deadly and was used long ago as a form of merciful execution. Pressure applied precisely causes the victim's neck to snap instantly.

TOS "JOURNEY TO BABEL"

Mok'bara Worf taught a class in this Klingon martial art while he served aboard the *Enterprise*-D. Some moves are similar to the Human discipline of tai chi chuan.

TNG "CLUES"

Galeo-Manada An alien style of wrestling, Jadzia Dax enjoyed this brutal "but fun" sport that she felt made her more alert if she did it first thing in the morning.

DS9 "PLAYING GOD"

Suus Mahna A Vulcan discipline that takes years to master. T'Pol taught the colonists of a dilithium-mining planet the *Navorkot* technique that could help evade bladed attacks.

ENT "MARAUDERS"

Vulcan nerve pinch The peace-loving Vulcan race has an easy way to defend themselves from less-logical species. Their method of pinching a humanoid at a nerve cluster at the base of the neck usually renders any victim unconscious.

TOS "THE ENEMY WITHIN"

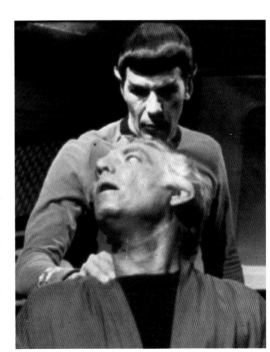

As the misquoted saying goes, music soothes the savage beast—and in space there are a lot of savage and not-so-savage species. It's good to keep a song in your heart, or at least, a vocal subprocessor and universal translator handy, when traveling through the Galaxy. Here's a playlist suitable for any road trip to the stars . . .

"Beyond Antares" . . . . TOS "THE CONSCIENCE OF THE KING"/"THE CHANGELING"

"The Good Land" and **"Heading Out to Eden"** (A space hippie medley) . . . . . . TOS "THE WAY TO EDEN"

"Row, Row, Row Your Boat" . . . . *STAR TREK V: THE FINAL FRONTIER*

"Pop Goes the Weasel" . . . . TNG "ENCOUNTER AT FARPOINT"/"BROTHERS"

"Frères Jacques" . . . . TNG "DISASTER"

"Magic Carpet Ride" . . . . *STAR TREK: FIRST CONTACT*

"A British Tar" . . . . *STAR TREK: INSURRECTION*

Aktuh and Melota (Klingon opera) . . . . . . TNG "UNIFICATION"/DS9 "LOOKING FOR *PAR'MACH* IN ALL THE WRONG PLACES"

"It's Only a Paper Moon" . . . . DS9 "IT'S ONLY A PAPER MOON"

"You Are My Sunshine" . . . . VGR "SOMEONE TO WATCH OVER ME"

"La donna è mobile" . . . . VGR "TINKER TENOR DOCTOR SPY"/"VIRTUOSO"

"Where My Heart Will Take Me" . . . . ENT

"Sabotage" . . . . *STAR TREK* (2009)/*STAR TREK BEYOND*

"Sledgehammer" . . . . *STAR TREK BEYOND*

Q-BIQUITOUS

If a god can be anywhere and everywhere, it did appear that Q—a member of the nearly omnipotent Q Continuum—was godlike in his abilities. He seemed to have a special fondness for humanity, appearing often to Starfleet Captains Picard, Sisko, and Janeway. Arrogant and condescending, Q bedeviled Picard more than any other Starfleet officer, but ultimately proved to be an odd sort of ally. Still, some of his antics caused nothing but trouble.

"Encounter at Farpoint" Q materialized to proclaim to the *Enterprise*-D crew that humanity was too savage to travel the stars and placed it on trial. He used Picard's crew as representatives of all Terrans. They passed the test that Q gave them, but he warned he would be watching. TNG

"Hide and Q" In an attempt to understand the Human qualities of wanting to grow, Q granted Riker some of the Q powers until Picard won a bet with Q and forced him back to the Continuum. TNG

"Q Who" Kicked out of the Continuum for his actions, Q requested to join Picard's crew. He claimed they would need him to fight the threats that lay ahead. When Picard refused, Q hurled the ship into Borg space—causing the two races to meet well before their time. TNG

"Deja Q" Stripped of his powers by the Q Continuum, Q took refuge on the *Enterprise*-D. After nearly causing Data's death, Q left to spare the crew further attacks. This unselfish act brought another member of the Continuum to his side who restored his powers and position. TNG

"Qpid" Wanting to repay Picard for his help in returning him to the Continuum, Q reunited the captain with his former lover, Vash. Placing the crew in a scenario based on Robin Hood, Q thought that would teach Picard a lesson in love. Ultimately, fascinated with Q, Vash left to travel with him for a time. TNG

"True Q" Q appeared to initiate a new Q in Amanda Rogers, a girl raised as Human by her Q parents who had abandoned the Continuum. She fought him, but realized her developing powers needed the guidance of her people. TNG

"Q-Less" Q encountered Sisko when he deposited Vash on Deep Space 9 after she tired of traveling with him. Punches were exchanged, and Q wound up flat on his back at the hands of a captain with less patience for his antics than Picard. DS9

"Tapestry" Acting as a guardian angel, Q showed a mortally injured Picard what his life might have been like after changing a crucial moment in the captain's personal timeline. TNG

"All Good Things . . ." As an anti-time paradox threatened the human race, Q claimed it was part of the trial of humanity. He judged them guilty of being inferior. In fact, it was a test devised by the Continuum to gauge Humans' capability to expand their horizons. Helping Picard was Q's own idea. TNG

"Death Wish" After the *Voyager* crew accidentally freed a renegade Q, the Continuum sent the one-and-only original Q to prevent the renegade (now calling himself "Quinn") from committing suicide. Swayed by Quinn, Q assisted him in his wish. VGR

"The Q and the Grey" Quinn's death plunged the Q Continuum into civil war, with Q leading a faction for change. He proposed creating a new half-Human breed of Q, by mating with Janeway. She opposed the idea, though she and the crew helped him in the war. He ended up mating with his old love, a female Q, and the first new Q in millennia was born in the Continuum. VGR

"Q2" Neither Q appeared to be a good parent, as Q Junior grew to be a spoiled brat. Q left him on *Voyager* to teach him a lesson, but Janeway convinced him the work of parenting needed to be done by Q himself. He reluctantly agreed. VGR

WISH YOU WERE HERE!

As more and more strange new worlds were explored by Starfleet, some stood out for their culture, their beauty, their uniqueness, or even their danger. While not every planet was a vacation paradise, some of the most notable planets in the Galaxy include:

Risa Perhaps the ultimate vacation spot, Risa is known as a pleasure planet. Orbiting a binary star about ninety light-years from Earth, the planet was once geologically unstable and it rained there constantly. Weather and seismic technology transformed the planet and now landmarks like Suraya Bay and Temtibi Lagoon serve tourists from all over the Galaxy.

TNG "CAPTAIN'S HOLIDAY"/
DS9 "LET HE WHO IS WITHOUT SIN"

Andoria M-class moon in orbit of the planet Andor. Andoria is home to founding Federation members, the blue-skinned Andorians. It is an icy world where temperatures rarely rise above freezing. The atmosphere is an oxygen-nitrogen mix that Humans are able to breathe. The Aenar, a subspecies of Andorians, live in the Northern Wastes.

ENT "THE AENAR"

Vulcan The predominantly desert world was a founding member of the United Federation of Planets. With its thinner atmosphere, higher gravity, and hot temperature, Humans are not always comfortable on Vulcan, which is about sixteen light-years from Earth. Notable landmarks include Mount Seleya, the Fire Plains and Vulcan's Forge. In the *Kelvin* Timeline, Nero caused the planet's destruction, with only 10,000 Vulcans able to evacuate their homeworld.

TOS "AMOK TIME" /
ENT "THE ANDORIAN INCIDENT" / "THE FORGE"
STAR TREK III: THE SEARCH FOR SPOCK / STAR TREK (2009)

Qo'noS The Klingon homeworld is an M-Class planet in the Beta Quadrant with one moon, Praxis. Home of a warrior race, the Klingon Empire held sway over many planets and was antagonistic to the Federation. When Praxis, the Klingon moon, exploded, it caused intense damage to the planet's ecosystem, which led to the Klingons reaching an accord with the Federation. Key features of the planet include the Kri'stak volcano, where legend told Kahless the Unforgettable forged the first *bat'leth* from dipping his hair in lava.

STAR TREK VI: THE UNDISCOVERED COUNTRY/
TNG "RIGHTFUL HEIR"

Bajor Like Earth, Bajor features geographic varieties of terrain like mountains, forests, and plains. The eleventh planet in its system, Bajor was invaded and occupied by the Cardassian Union for fifty years. Both the population and planet suffered greatly with untold numbers dying as the people were enslaved. Once the Cardassians withdrew, the Federation assisted in helping the Bajorans renew and recover their planet. A famous landmark is the Fire Caves, where the Pah-wraiths were imprisoned.

DS9 "EMISSARY"/ "WHAT YOU LEAVE BEHIND"

Romulus and Remus Twin planets in Sector Z-6, Romulus was colonized by a group of Vulcans during Earth's fourth century. While Romulus was a temperate planet, Remus was tidally locked, so that one side always faced the star it orbited. Remans lived only on the night side and were sensitive to light. Gal Gath'thong on Romulus was an area known for its spectacular firefalls. Romulus (and possibly Remus as well) was destroyed by a singularity in 2367.

TNG "THE DEFECTOR"/ "GAMBIT"/
STAR TREK NEMESIS/ STAR TREK (2009)

Cardassia Prime Scarcity of resources on the capital world of the Cardassian Union caused its society to become militaristic. It then relied on conquest and plunder to stay strong. The planet suffered the loss of an entire city, Lakarian City, when Cardassia's Dominion allies leveled it in retaliation for resistance attacks on the planet's power systems.

TNG "CHAIN OF COMMAND"/
DS9 "FOR THE CAUSE"/"WHAT YOU LEAVE BEHIND"

THERE AND BACK AGAIN

Hodgkins's Law of Parallel Planetary Development states that planets with similar environments and population tend to develop in parallel biological and cultural ways. The crew of the *Enterprise* in The Original Series often visited planets that were extremely Earth-like. That helped the production with budgetary concerns, since visiting actual alien planets was cost prohibitive (and physically impossible) and building alien sets was also costly. These Earth-like planets, often populated by aliens who looked quite Human, allowed the writers to use their settings as an allegory to tell stories that hit a little closer to home for the audience.

Sigma Iotia II Before the institution of the Prime Directive, the *Horizon* landed on Sigma Iotia II and made first contact. The highly imitative population and its society became contaminated by a book left behind that became like a bible: *Chicago Mobs of the Twenties*. A violent and cold-blooded mob gang culture evolved. Kirk played by the mob "rules" and developed a syndicate where the Federation would be the "boss" and their cut of all profits would administer Federation action to guide the Iotians to a more ethical societal system.

TOS "A PIECE OF THE ACTION"

Miri's World An almost exact duplicate of Earth, even down to architectural styles and language, the biggest difference between this planet and the seat of the Federation was the makeup of the population. All the adults had died from a disease they accidentally unleashed. Only the centuries-old children still lived, until they hit puberty and would die. The disease began to affect the landing party, though McCoy found a cure and left a team to care for the children until Starfleet could reach the planet and assist.

TOS "MIRI"

Miramanee's Planet The mysterious Wise Ones transplanted tribes of Native Americans to this M-Class planet prior to humanity discovering space travel. The planet allowed the tribes to continue their culture. Though asteroids threatened the planet, the Wise Ones had left a deflector, which malfunctioned until Kirk and his crew were able to repair it.

TOS "THE PARADISE SYNDROME"

Omega IV An example of culture contamination and parallel development can be found in Omega IV. The planet was devastated by biological warfare a thousand years prior to the *Enterprise* crew's visit. Two groups, the Yangs and Kohms, were remarkably similar to Americans and Asians on Earth. The Yangs even worshiped an American flag and a constitution. When Captain Ronald Tracey lost his crew to a virus that existed on Omega IV, he violated the Prime Directive to help the Kohms fight the Yangs in order to find the secret to their longevity.

TOS "THE OMEGA GLORY"

Planet 892-IV An M-Class planet whose society developed its own Roman Empire, which never fell. Their technology was similar to Earth's in the twentieth century with the equivalent of television and motor vehicles. The society itself remained primitive, with slavery still in existence and gladiatorial fights to the death televised as entertainment. Monitored broadcasts showed that parallels between Earth's Christianity might still cause the empire's fall.

TOS "BREAD AND CIRCUSES"

Ekos While not a planet that evolved like Earth naturally, the reason for the Federation's Prime Directive of noninterference in primitive cultures was seen here. Historian John Gill attempted to help the chaotic society of Ekos by applying principles of the National Socialist Party to it but ended up recreating the Nazi movement. As Gill died, he realized how power corrupts. His successor Eneg appeared ready to end the fascist way they'd lived.

TOS "PATTERNS OF FORCE"

COSMIC PHENOMENON

Space is mostly an empty void, with stars and planets making up little of its mass. But there's a lot more than matter and energy out there. As humanity reached for the stars, it found that extraordinary stellar phenomena like supernovas and comets paled in comparison to some of the cosmic anomalies in the Galaxy.

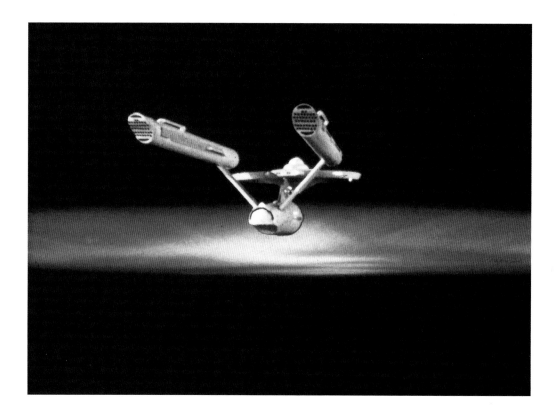

Galactic Barrier This negative energy force field surrounds the Milky Way Galaxy. Travel through the barrier is dangerous and during the *Enterprise*'s first encounter with the phenomenon, two members of the crew gained immense psionic powers.

TOS "WHERE NO MAN HAS GONE BEFORE"/
"BY ANY OTHER NAME"/
"IS THERE IN TRUTH NO BEAUTY?"

Quantum Fissure Worf encountered a quantum fissure on his way back to the *Enterprise*-D, returning from a *bat'leth* tournament, and he soon found himself briefly intersecting with numerous realities. In one, the Borg had conquered the Federation while in another the Bajorans conquered the Cardassians and in several others Worf was married to Counselor Troi.

TNG "PARALLELS"

Q Continuum The other-dimensional home of the near-omnipotent beings known as the Q, the Continuum also refers to the entire race of people. Janeway and members of her crew are the only Humans to have visited the Continuum, which they did on two separate occasions.

TNG "ENCOUNTER AT FARPOINT" /
VGR "DEATH WISH" / "THE Q AND THE GREY"

Iconian Gateway The ancient Iconians were known as the "Demons of Air and Darkness," presumably for their ability to appear from nowhere through their galaxy-spanning gateways. These devices let a user step through a door-shaped portal to another portal, up to at least 70,000 light-years away. Only two gateways were known to exist and both were destroyed to prevent future use.

TNG "CONTAGION" /
DS9 "TO THE DEATH"

Badlands Partially situated in the Demilitarized Zone between Federation and Cardassian space, the area is known for intense plasma storms and gravitational anomalies. This made it a logical hiding place for the Maquis to stage raids and attacks on the Cardassians.

DS9 "THE MAQUIS" /
VGR "CARETAKER"

The Void An odd, donut-shaped inert layer of subspace in the Delta Quadrant with funnels that occasionally extruded into regular space became known to the *Voyager* crew as "the Void." These funnels capture ships, trapping them in this area of space that has no stars, no planets, and no matter of any kind.

VGR "THE VOID"

Nexus Every 39.1 years, a ribbon of temporal energy known as the Nexus sweeps through the Galaxy. Inside the Nexus, a person's wishes and fondest desires take shape.

STAR TREK GENERATIONS

Celestial Temple The wormhole that connects the Alpha and Gamma Quadrants in the Denorios belt of the Bajoran system was possibly the first known stable wormhole. Bajoran legends had long suspected what they called a Celestial Temple existed near their planet. The noncorporeal Prophets of Bajoran legend live within the wormhole while also existing outside of space and time.

DS9 "EMISSARY" / "WHAT YOU LEAVE BEHIND"

Delphic Expanse The transdimensional entities known as the Sphere-Builders created seventy-eight Spheres that formed an area two-thousand light-years wide known as the Delphic Expanse. The Expanse was covered in thermobaric clouds and contained a web of gravimetric anomalies. Essentially, the Spheres were making space more habitable for the Builders' species. The Spheres and the Expanse were destroyed by the crew of *Enterprise* NX-01.

ENT "THE EXPANSE" / "ZERO HOUR"

Briar Patch Named for the Brer Rabbit stories written by Joel Chandler Harris of Earth, the area contains the remains of supernovae. The Ba'ku people settled on a planet within the Briar Patch, where the metaphysic radiation rejuvenates their cells and prolongs their life span.

DS9 "BLOOD OATH" / *STAR TREK: INSURRECTION*

Mirror Universe Starfleet personnel have either visited this parallel universe where basic evil replaces basic good or they have encountered their dark duplicates from this place. The United Federation of Planets does not exist in this Universe, instead, the Terran Empire was the main spacefaring power in the Alpha Quadrant until a Klingon-Cardassian Alliance replaced it.

TOS "MIRROR, MIRROR"
DS9 "CROSSOVER" / "THROUGH THE LOOKING GLASS" /
ENT "IN A MIRROR, DARKLY"

COSMIC CREATURES

TRAVELING IN SPACE MEANS HAVING TO ADJUST TO A LARGER SCALE WHERE DISTANCE, TIME, AND EVEN LIFE-FORMS CAN BE ENORMOUS. WHILE SOME NONCORPOREAL LIFE-FORMS CAN APPEAR HUGE, THERE ARE SOME CREATURES THAT ARE BORN GIGANTIC AND JUST GET BIGGER.

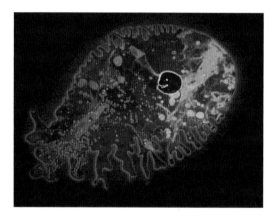

Space Amoeba Perhaps one of the largest and most bizarre life-forms Captain Kirk and the *Enterprise* crew encountered was a gigantic space amoeba. A single-celled organism over eleven thousand miles in length, it drained energy from starships and organic life.

TOS "THE IMMUNITY SYNDROME"

Farpoint Entities On the maiden voyage of the *Enterprise*-D, the crew investigated Farpoint Station, which was constructed by the inhabitants of Deneb IV. The station turned out to be an injured intelligent creature forced to morph into the base, and an attacking spacecraft was revealed to be the creature's mate, trying to free it.

TNG "ENCOUNTER AT FARPOINT"

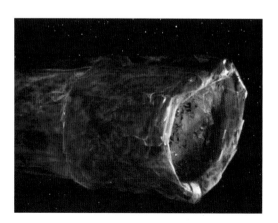

Doomsday Machine The cone-shaped planet-killer used an antiproton beam to break down planets into fuel, and could decimate an entire system.

TOS "THE DOOMSDAY MACHINE"

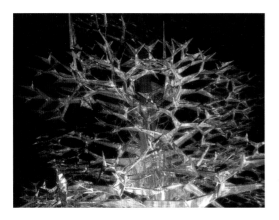

Crystalline Entity Similar in structure to a snowflake, the enormous Crystalline Entity traveled through space to collect electromagnetic power, converting organic matter to energy that it fed on.

TNG "DATALORE"/"SILICON AVATAR"

"Junior" The creature nicknamed "Junior" was born when the *Enterprise*-D helped perform a Caesarean section by phaser on its dying mother. A life-form the size of a four-story building, Junior attached itself to the *Enterprise* and drained power, apparently feeding off the fusion generators.

TNG "GALAXY'S CHILD"

Class-J Nebula Lifeform When the *U.S.S. Voyager* gathered deuterium from a Class-J nebula, that nebula began to destabilize because it was actually a life-form, which soon attempted to take over *Voyager*. It attempted to change the ship's environment to resemble its own while it forced the ship to reverse course and take it home.

VGR "THE HAUNTING OF DECK TWELVE"

Nagilum The immortal being from outside the universe had no distinct form, but its intelligence was believed to be vast. It had curiosity in the "limited existence" of humanoids that it wanted to explore, murdering a member of the *Enterprise*-D crew and threatening the ship.

TNG "WHERE SILENCE HAS LEASE"

GREAT MINDS THINK ALIKE

THE VULCAN ABILITY TO TELEPATHICALLY MERGE TWO CONSCIENCES WITH A MIND-MELD WAS ONCE CONSIDERED DEVIANT, AS MANY OF THEIR PEOPLE BELIEVED ONLY A MINORITY OF THEIR RACE WERE BORN WITH THE POWER. EVENTUALLY IT BECAME MORE ACCEPTABLE, BUT STILL A DEEPLY INTIMATE EXPERIENCE, ONE MOST VULCANS AVOIDED PERFORMING WITH OFF-WORLDERS. HOWEVER, BECAUSE TWO MINDS ARE OFTEN BETTER THAN ONE IN SPACE TRAVEL, MANY SITUATIONS AROSE THAT CREATED THE NEED FOR THE DEEPLY PERSONAL SHARED EXPERIENCE.

Spock/Horta Spock successfully melded with a silicon-based life-form, the Horta, to understand why it was killing miners.

TOS "THE DEVIL IN THE DARK"

Spock/Nomad To find its origin, Spock melded with the alien probe's intelligence.

TOS "THE CHANGELING"

Mirror Spock/McCoy The "evil" universe version of Spock forcibly melded with McCoy to discover the doctor's origin.

TOS "MIRROR, MIRROR"

Miranda Jones/Spock Spock accidentally saw the Medusan ambassador Kollos's true form and it drove him insane. Jones, a telepath who'd studied on Vulcan, was able to restore his mind.

TOS "IS THERE IN TRUTH NO BEAUTY"

Spock/Kirk When Kirk's mind was trapped in the body of former lover Janice Lester, Spock was able to verify the fact.

TOS "TURNABOUT INTRUDER"

Spock/V'Ger Spock melded with the giant probe to understand its origins.

STAR TREK: THE MOTION PICTURE

Spock/McCoy The dying Spock transferred his *katra*, or soul, to McCoy.

STAR TREK II: THE WRATH OF KHAN

Spock/George and Gracie After time-traveling to 1986, Spock jumped into a tank and melded with two humpback whales to see if they would come to the future and help the *Enterprise* crew save Earth.

STAR TREK IV: THE VOYAGE HOME

Spock/Valeris Disappointed by his protégé's involvement with a conspiracy to sabotage the Khitomer peace talks, Spock forcibly entered her mind to find who was behind the plot.

STAR TREK VI: THE UNDISCOVERED COUNTRY

Sarek/Picard Unable to perform negotiations due to being stricken by Bendii syndrome, Sarek's last diplomatic mission seemed doomed to failure until Picard volunteered to mind-meld with him to stabilize the ambassador.

TNG "SAREK"

Spock/Picard After his father died, Spock expressed regret that he'd never had the chance to meld with his father. Picard offered to meld with Spock so he could share what the captain had experienced during his earlier meld with Sarek.

TNG "UNIFICATION, PART II"

Sakonna/Dukat The Vulcan Maquis was unable to penetrate Dukat's mind because the Cardassian claimed his mental disciplines allowed him to resist her.

DS9 "THE MAQUIS"

Tuvok/Lon Suder Tuvok melded with Suder to help the Betazoid sociopath control his emotions, but it had the opposite effect on Tuvok.

VGR "MELD"

Tuvok/Janeway Tuvok melded with Janeway to find the cause of a memory virus. Together they relived some of his time under Captain Sulu's command and discovered the source of the virus.

VGR "FLASHBACK"

Tolaris/T'Pol An improperly performed mind-meld caused T'Pol to later develop Pa'nar Syndrome.

ENT "FUSION"/"KIR'SHARA"

Mirror T'Pol/Mirror Tucker In the mirror universe, T'Pol ordered Tucker to sabotage the *I.S.S. Enterprise*, then removed his memory of doing so.

ENT "IN A MIRROR, DARKLY"

Spock Prime/Kirk In the *Kelvin* Timeline, the aged Spock melded with Kirk to show him how the alternate reality came to be.

STAR TREK (2009)

OF GODS AND MEN

THE FEDERATION SUPPORTS ALL KINDS OF FAITHS, BUT IT MAINTAINS AN ADHERENCE TO SCIENCE AS THE FOUNDATION OF ITS POLICIES. MOST ANY PHENOMENON COULD BE EXPLAINED BY SCIENCE, EVEN IF IT SEEMED LIKE MAGIC. AS STARFLEET BEGAN TO SPREAD ACROSS THE GALAXY, ITS PERSONNEL ENCOUNTERED MORE AND MORE OMNIPOTENT (AND NEAR-OMNIPOTENT) BEINGS WITH PHYSICS-DEFYING POWERS.

Q The immortal members of the Q Continuum demonstrated incredible power each time they encountered Starfleet personnel. They can create energy barriers in space, rearrange matter, travel or send people through time, and shunt a starship thousands of light-years through space. Only members of the Continuum have the ability to punish or negate a Q's powers and abilities.

TNG "ENCOUNTER AT FARPOINT"/"Q WHO"

Charlie Evans Orphaned after his parents crashed on the inhospitable planet Thasus, Charlie was raised by the noncorporeal Thasians, and gifted with incredible powers to help him survive. He could create, destroy, or rearrange matter, had telepathic and telekinetic powers, and could control people's minds.

TOS "CHARLIE X"

Prophets For 30,000 years, the Bajorans had visions and legends of the Prophets—blue, energy-like aliens living inside the stable wormhole that created the powerful Orbs at the cornerstone of the Bajoran religion. Benjamin Sisko, or simply "the Sisko" as the Prophets called him, was revealed to be their Emissary, who would help vanquish their ancient enemies, the Pah-wraiths.

DS9 "EMISSARY"/"WHAT YOU LEAVE BEHIND"

"God" The god entity imprisoned in the Great Barrier at the center of the Galaxy was not a god at all, but a powerful noncorporeal being that needed a starship to help him escape his prison.

STAR TREK V: THE FINAL FRONTIER

Blessed Exchequer While no one has yet encountered the avatar of the Ferengi belief system, every good Ferengi prays to this semidivine entity. In order to enter the Divine Treasury and bid on new lives, a Ferengi has to have their balance sheets in order to present to the Blessed Exchequer. If their balance is negative, the Ferengi souls are sentenced to the Vault of Eternal Destitution.

DS9 "LITTLE GREEN MEN"

Apollo An alien who claimed to be the Greek god Apollo encountered the *Enterprise* crew on Pollux IV, causing anthropology officer Carolyn Palamas to reason that the ancient gods of Earth were actually space travelers with incredible powers. Apollo could grow in size, rearrange matter, summon bolts of lightning, and he even generated a force field shaped like a hand to stop the *Enterprise* in flight. His powers came from an extra organ in his chest that tapped into an energy generator in his temple.

TOS "WHO MOURNS FOR ADONAIS"

Trelane The self-styled Squire of Gothos appeared to be an adult to the *Enterprise* crew, but he was essentially a child. Trelane had tremendous powers, including the ability to make planets. Like any child, he was unable to escape the discipline of his parents, who appeared to the *Enterprise* crew as flashing green lights.

TOS "THE SQUIRE OF GOTHOS"

D'Arsay Archive The immensely powerful data storage archive found in a rogue comet was not alive, but it physically transformed parts of the *Enterprise*-D, manipulating matter (and Data) into bringing characters from its culture to life.

TNG "MASKS"

Pah-wraiths While the wormhole-dwelling aliens known as the Prophets were mostly benevolent, some committed acts of evil. Those were punished and sentenced to exile in Bajor's Fire Caves.

DS9 "THE ASSIGNMENT"/"THE RECKONING"

Sphere Builders The Xindi races worshiped transdimensional beings known only as the Guardians. This highly advanced race had the ability to see alternate timelines and manipulate events to their advantage. Unable to live in normal space, they built the spheres to transform a large area into the Delphic Expanse, which was more suitable for their race.

ENT "THE COUNCIL"/"CHOSEN REALM"

YOU WILL BE ASSIMILATED

IF PRACTICE MAKES PERFECT, THE BORG ATTEMPT TO PUT THAT SAYING TO THE TEST IN THEIR QUEST TO PERFECT THEIR COLLECTIVE. THEY PRACTICE THEIR GOAL OF CREATING A PERFECT BLEND OF ORGANIC AND SYNTHETIC LIFE BY ASSIMILATING ALMOST EVERY SPECIES THEY ENCOUNTER. CONNECTED TO A HIVE MIND, THE ONLY MEMBER OF THEIR RACE WITH INDIVIDUALITY WITHIN THE COLLECTIVE IS THE BORG QUEEN. SHE FUNCTIONED SIMILARLY TO A QUEEN BEE, DIRECTING DRONES AND BRINGING ORDER TO THE COLLECTIVE AND, HOPEFULLY, BEYOND. TO THAT END, THE BORG MADE SEVERAL INCURSIONS AGAINST STARFLEET PERSONNEL, INCLUDING:

System J-25 Captain Picard and crew first encountered the Borg outside of their own quadrant, when Q flung them seven thousand light-years from home. They saw a distinctive cube-shaped Borg ship after it scooped entire industrialized cities off an M-Class planet. The Borg boarded the *Enterprise*-D, then gave chase. Picard had to appeal to Q's vanity to get them back to their own space but, as Guinan warned, the Borg now knew humanity existed.

TNG "Q WHO"

Argolis Cluster The *Enterprise*-D discovered a crashed Borg scout ship with a critically injured adolescent Borg on board. While he recovered, an embittered Picard wanted to use the drone as a Trojan Horse weapon against the Collective. The Borg gradually reclaimed his individuality and a name: Hugh. Ultimately, Picard chose not to use Hugh as a weapon, though the drone voluntarily went back to the Collective to protect his new friends.

TNG "I, BORG"

Lore's Planet Hugh's individuality proved to be as disruptive to the Collective as any virus Picard could have implanted. His entire cube fell into chaos as his shared experiences spread confusion. The Collective cut them off and they drifted until Data's brother Lore gave them a new sense of purpose and led them against the *Enterprise* crew. Hugh and drones loyal to him helped defeat Lore.

TNG "DESCENT"

Unicomplex Admiral Janeway from the future traveled back to the past version of herself still traveling in the Delta Quadrant. Together, they implemented the admiral's plan to be assimilated and release a pathogen that would cause the Borg Queen's death. This enabled *Voyager* to return to the Alpha Quadrant through the Borg transwarp network years earlier than in the Admiral's time.

VGR "ENDGAME"

Bozeman, Montana The Borg traveled back in time to attempt to stop Earth's first warp-drive flight and subsequent first contact with the Vulcan race. The *Enterprise*-E followed the Borg ship back in time and encountered historical figure Zefram Cochrane. Data and Picard were kidnapped and Picard came face-to-face with the Borg Queen. They managed to kill this aspect of the Queen and ensure history proceeded as intended.

STAR TREK: FIRST CONTACT

Fluidic Space When Species 8472 began attacking the Borg and *Voyager* from their domain in fluidic space, Janeway saw only one option: an alliance with the Federation's most dangerous enemies. When the alliance ended, *Voyager* gained a new crew member in the reluctant former drone, Seven of Nine.

VGR "SCORPION"

Borg Queen's Vessel Captain Janeway encountered the Borg Queen and learned that it was she who let Seven of Nine be taken by *Voyager* two years earlier. The Queen planned to reintegrate Seven and increase her own perfection, but Janeway foiled the plan.

VGR "UNIMATRIX ZERO"

New Providence/Wolf 359 Starfleet created a task force to plan against a coming invasion, but they were still unprepared when the colony of New Providence was ripped away by the Borg. The *Enterprise*-D went after the Borg, only to see Picard captured, assimilated, and help the Borg damage the *Enterprise*. After the ship was repaired, they made their way to join a fleet of Starfleet and Klingon vessels at Wolf 359, but arrived too late. The fleet had been destroyed, leading to the deaths of thousands, including the wife of Benjamin Sisko. As the Borg cube headed for Earth, the crew managed to recapture Picard, who provided a clue to temporarily defeating the Borg.

TNG "THE BEST OF BOTH WORLDS"

THE SEVEN-YEAR ITCH

Vulcans prize logic over emotion, knowing it saved their civilization. The ancient Vulcans endured a barbaric way of life, and their savagery almost destroyed them. Surak, the father of Vulcan philosophy, led them through it to the Time of Awakening where the entire race worked to purge their passionate nature and embrace logic. While Vulcans still feel emotions, they suppress them completely. Consequently, Vulcan customs are unlike almost any others in the Galaxy and can appear odd to those who do not comprehend the intellectual joy of total logic.

Greeting The traditional Vulcan greeting is to raise a hand, palm outward, and create a V-shape between the middle and index fingers. Often it begins by one saying "Peace and long life" and the response is the more famous "Live long and prosper."

TOS "AMOK TIME"

Vulcan Affection Vulcans are never so vulgar in their displays of affection. Mates express their love with a simple caress on the hand of the other using a dignified two-finger tracing motion.

TOS "JOURNEY TO BABEL"

Vulcan Neuropressure This ritual is a heightened form of massage that also involves stimulating neural nodes and pressure points, while engaging in breathing exercises. The techniques are challenging to learn and master.

ENT "THE XINDI"

Kahs-wan This grueling survival test of maturity challenges a pre-teen Vulcan to survive in the harsh landscape of Vulcan's Forge for ten days without water, food, or weapons.

TAS "YESTERYEAR"/ENT "THE CATWALK"

Fal-tor-pan A risky ritual that rejoins the *katra* transferred from a person back into their body. When the Genesis effect rejuvenated the dead Spock's body, Vulcan High priestess T'Lar was able to return Spock's *katra* from McCoy with the near-mindless body.

STAR TREK III: THE SEARCH FOR SPOCK

Kolinahr Most Vulcans choose not to undergo this extreme ritual of completely purging all emotion. It can take from two to six years to master and usually requires semi-isolation in a monastery to achieve.

STAR TREK: THE MOTION PICTURE

Vulcan Mind-Meld The joining of two minds was considered offensive for centuries, though by the twenty-third century, it was no longer a stigma among Vulcans.

ENT "STIGMA"

Pon farr and ***plak tow*** Vulcans mate only once every seven years. At the time the mating urges begin, a Vulcan's neurochemistry becomes so unbalanced they could die within eight days if their urges are not satiated. The final stage of *Pon farr* is *plak tow*, or "blood fever." At this point, the Vulcan is irrational and sometimes has trouble speaking. Aside from taking a mate, the only other options for Vulcans are intensive meditation and the *kal-if-fee* or a fight to the death.

TOS "AMOK TIME"/
VGR "BLOOD FEVER"

Katra Vulcans believe the *katra* is essentially their living spirit that lives on after death if transferred properly. Katric arks are said to be vessels for those spirits, though none yet have been found to contain a *katra*. Surak's *katra* survived from the Time of Awakening and briefly resided in Captain Archer's mind. When Spock died of radiation poisoning, he transferred his *katra* to Dr. McCoy, until it could be reunited with his regenerated body.

STAR TREK II: THE WRATH OF KHAN/
ENT "THE FORGE"

IDIC "Infinite Diversity in Infinite Combinations" is a conerstone of the Vulcan belief system.

TOS "IS THERE IN TRUTH NO BEAUTY"

Chapter 3

SHIPS AND TECHNOLOGY OF THE FUTURE

It IS Rocket Science!

LIST #39
TONGUE-TWISTING TECHNOBABBLE

ACTING IN A *STAR TREK* FILM OR EPISODE CAN BE A GREAT BOOST FOR AN ACTOR'S CAREER, BUT MANY DREAD THE AMOUNT OF PSEUDOSCIENTIFIC LINGO OR "TECHNOBABBLE" IN THE SCRIPTS. WHILE SERIES REGULARS WHO DEAL WITH MEDICAL AND ENGINEERING OFTEN GET THE WORST OF IT, SOMETIMES GUEST STARS ALSO HAVE TO ATTEMPT TO CONVEY A REALISTIC MEANING BEHIND CHALLENGING WORDS AND PHRASES. A FULL LIST OF TECHNOBABBLE USED THROUGHOUT THE SERIES COULD FILL KILOQUADS OF VERBIAGE PRINTED ON FLATTENED SHEETS OF CELLULOSE PULP, BUT HERE'S A TINY TASTE OF THE TONGUE-TWISTIEST TECHNOBABBLE . . .

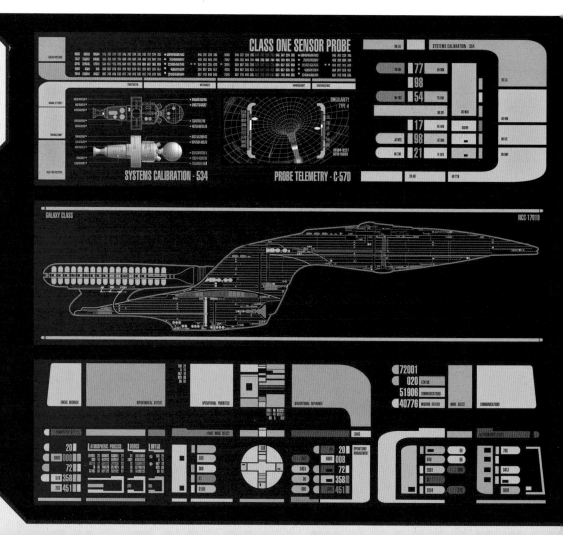

"Tell me, are you using a polymer-based neuro-relay to transmit the organic nerve impulses to the central processor of my positronic net? If that is the case, how have you solved the problem of increased signal degradation inherent to organo-synthetic transfer—"

DATA, *STAR TREK: FIRST CONTACT*

". . . The *Enterprise* computer system is controlled by three primary main processing cores cross-linked with a redundant melacortz ramistat and fourteen kiloquad interface modules. The core elements are based on FTL nanoprocessor units arranged into twenty-five bilateral kelilactirals with twenty of those units being slaved to the central heisenfram terminal. . . . You do know what a bilateral kelilactiral is, don't you?"

RIKER, TNG "RASCALS"

"After we launch our target drone, the *Defiant* will have to generate a subspace tensor matrix in the twenty-five to thirty thousand Cochrane range. Then the drone will send out a magneton pulse, which should react with the matrix to create an opening in the space-time continuum."

TRILL SCIENTIST BEJAL OTNER, DS9 "REJOINED"

". . . The phase inducers are connected to the emitter array. The override is completely gone, and the pattern buffer's been locked into a continuous diagnostic cycle."

LA FORGE, TNG "RELICS"

"The secondary gyrodyne relays and the propulsion field intermatrix have depolarized."

EMH MARK II, VGR "MESSAGE IN A BOTTLE"

BASHIR: It's heresy to even consider the possibility that prion replication could be inhibited by quantum resonance effects. Aren't you going to take any notes?

JAKE: Good idea.

BASHIR: According to the so-called experts, it's all a matter of amino acid resequencing and disulfide shuffling. Quantum dynamics has nothing to do with it.

DS9 "NOR THE BATTLE TO THE STRONG"

". . . The Tamarians are projecting a particle-sustaining beam into the upper atmosphere. The result is a hyperionisation that virtually disrupts all EM and subspace carriers."

DATA, TNG "DARMOK"

". . . It's a simple matter of extracting the iconometric elements, and triaxilating a recursion matrix."

ARTURIS, VGR "HOPE AND FEAR"

"Picard and his lackeys would have solved all this technobabble hours ago. No wonder you're not commanding a starship."

Q, "Q-LESS"

Of course, not all technobabble requires big words . . .

"One-seven-three-four-six-seven-three-two-one-four-seven-six-Charlie-three-two-seven-eight-nine-seven-seven-six-four-three-Tango-seven-three-two-Victor-seven-three-one-one-seven-eight-eight-eight-seven-three-two-four-seven-six-seven-eight-nine-seven-six-four-three-seven-six. Lock." Data locks out the computer with an encrypted password even your IT department would approve of in TNG "Brothers"

FULLY IMMERSIVE ENTERTAINMENT

FROM RADIO TO BLU-RAY, FROM *THE OREGON TRAIL* TO *WORLD OF WARCRAFT*, HUMANS LOSE THEMSELVES IN THE STORIES THEY CREATE AND SHARE. IN THE TWENTY-FOURTH CENTURY, TECHNOLOGY ADVANCED TO THE POINT THAT A ROOM FILLED WITH HOLOGRAPHIC EMITTERS COULD CREATE ANY ENVIRONMENT FOR PERSONAL ENTERTAINMENT. SOME OF THE MORE POPULAR PROGRAMS INCLUDE:

Dixon Hill The Dixon Hill series of mysteries might be considered "holo-noir." Captain Picard enjoyed playing the role of fictional 1940s private investigator Dixon Hill. Some of the popular programs include "The Big Goodbye," "The Parrot's Claw," and "The Black Orchid."

TNG "THE BIG GOODBYE"/"MAN HUNT"

Barclay Program 15 The introverted Lieutenant Reginald Barclay had trouble with real people, but in the forests of Barclay Program 15 he had no trouble winning the woman he loved, and facing down musketeers and a much shorter Commander Riker.

TNG "HOLLOW PURSUITS"

Paris 3 One of the first programs Tom Paris added to *Voyager*'s holodeck was a French bar he spent a fair amount of time in when he studied at Starfleet Academy. Chez Sandrine's was frequented by members of the crew.

VGR "THE CLOUD"

Sherlock Holmes Program 3-A Data's attempt to create an adversary that could outwit him as he played the Sherlock Holmes holonovels resulted in the creation of a sentient Professor Moriarty hologram that wanted to escape his holodeck boundaries.

TNG "ELEMENTARY, DEAR DATA"/"SHIP IN A BOTTLE"

Baseball Field Sisko's love of baseball led him to accept a challenge to battle for the honor of Deep Space 9 out on the holo-field. He assembled the Niners to play Vulcan captain Solok's Logicians.

DS9 "TAKE ME OUT TO THE HOLOSUITE"

The Adventures of Flotter An educational holoprogram series designed for children shares the stories of Flotter the water elemental and his friends in the Forest of Forever. Their adventures include "Flotter and the Terribly Twisted Trunk" and "Flotter Meets the Invincible Invertebrates."

VGR "ONCE UPON A TIME"

Julian Bashir, Secret Agent Created by Bashir's friend Felix (who also designed Vic's Lounge), the Secret Agent series of holosuite programs are based on 1960s Earth-style spy stories. On one occasion, the holoprogram had to host the command crew's data patterns during an unusual transporter malfunction, and they literally became the outlandish characters in the story.

DS9 "OUR MAN BASHIR"

Vulcan Love Slave Based on the popular novel of the same name, Vulcan Love Slave was adapted into a holonovel that spawned several sequels.

DS9 "THE ASCENT"

The Adventures of Captain Proton Tom Paris's favorite holonovels were black-and-white homages to Earth's science-fiction movie serials of the 1930s. When photonic life-forms interacted with the program and confused reality for the holodeck, Janeway had to play her part as the "Bride of Chaotica!"

VGR "NIGHT"/"BRIDE OF CHAOTICA!"

Fair Haven Program Paris 042 Recreation of an Irish coastal town called Fair Haven. Janeway initially disliked the bartender, Michael Sullivan, but after tinkering with his program, she found herself falling for him. Eventually, she blocked her access to his behavior subroutines to avoid making that mistake again.

VGR "FAIR HAVEN"

Bashir-62 Also known as Vic's Lounge, the 1960s Vegas-style lounge is run by crooner Vic Fontaine. When the Dominion war ended, the Deep Space 9 crew gathered for a final celebration before many of them parted for new assignments.

DS9 "IT'S ONLY A PAPER MOON"/ "WHAT YOU LEAVE BEHIND"

da Vinci's Workshop Janeway went from captain to apprentice when she spent time in the holodeck simulation of Leonardo da Vinci's workshop in Italy. She helped him construct a flying glider that he designed and the pair got to test it on an alien world with the help of the Doctor's mobile emitter.

VGR "SCORPION"/"CONCERNING FLIGHT"

RELICS OF THE FUTURE

ARTIFACTS ARE TYPICALLY ITEMS OF CULTURAL OR HISTORICAL IMPORTANCE MADE BY HUMANS, OR AS STARFLEET PERSONNEL DISCOVERED AS THEY TRAVELED THE STARS, ALIENS. SOME OF THESE RELICS HAVE SURPRISING ABILITIES BEYOND CULTURAL SIGNIFICANCE TO THE RACES THAT CREATED THEM.

Sword of Kahless The first *bat'leth* ever forged was created by Kahless the Unforgettable. The great leader used it to carve a statue, kill a tyrant and a serpent, and to create an Empire. Its mythical symbolism among Klingons made it a dangerous object when it was found. When Worf realized this, he cast it out to drift in space.

TNG "RIGHTFUL HEIR"/DS9 "THE SWORD OF KAHLESS"

Spican Flame Gems Whether Spican flame gems have any value beyond their surface appearance is unknown. Both a Deep Space Station K-7 bartender and Captain Kirk declined to purchase any from Cyrano Jones.

TOS "THE TROUBLE WITH TRIBBLES"

Radan Necklace On the planet Troyius, radan is the name for dilithium, the rare substance that regulated the matter/antimatter flow in a starship's warp engine. Elaan, the Dolhman of Elas, had a necklace that Scotty was able to use to replace the fused crystals in the *Enterprise* engines after a Klingon attack.

TOS "ELAAN OF TROYIUS"

Sacred Chalice of Rixx One of the ceremonial artifacts Lwaxana Troi holds in her duties as a daughter of the Fifth House does have a name that sounds impressive. But her daughter, Deanna, confronted her privately that she did not hold it in as high esteem, as it was an "old clay pot with mold growing inside it."

TNG "MENAGE À TROI"

Stone of Gol A psionic resonator weapon created on Vulcan before they became a society based on logic could focus and amplify telepathic energy. Vulcan isolationists tried to acquire and reassemble the stone, but Picard stopped them and turned it over to the Vulcan authorities for destruction.

TNG "GAMBIT"

Jevonite Artifacts Before Cardassia Prime became a military culture, its First Hebitian Civilization created artifacts from the "breathtaking" stone, jevonite. Gul Madred owned a dagger with a jevonite handle.

TNG "CHAIN OF COMMAND"

Tox Uthat A powerful weapon from the 27th century, the Tox Uthat is a quantum phase inhibitor that can stop the nuclear fusion within a star, destroying it. Vorgon criminals tried to steal it from its inventor, who traveled back in time and hid it on the pleasure planet, Risa.

TNG "CAPTAIN'S HOLIDAY"

Kurlan Naiskos This hollow ceramic figurine of the ancient Kurlan civilization hides a number of smaller figurines inside, representing the philosophy that the individual is part of a larger community of individuals with distinct voices. Captain Picard received one as a gift from Professor Richard Galen.

TNG "THE CHASE"

Orbs of the Prophets Created by the wormhole-dwelling aliens known as the Prophets, the Orbs are tangible energy fields that offer visions or hallucinatory insights to the past, present, or future. Monks keep the orbs safe in jeweled vessels. Nine in all, the Orbs named by the Bajoran people included the Orb of Prophecy and Change, the Orb of Time, and the Orb of Contemplation.

DS9 "EMISSARY"

INSPIRED BY THE FUTURE

MUCH OF THE TECHNOLOGY WE ENJOY TODAY CAN BE TRACED DIRECTLY TO THE VISIONS OF FUTURE APPLIED SCIENCE SEEN IN *STAR TREK* WITH INCREDIBLE LEAPS IN FIELDS THAT, LIKE ALL GREAT SCIENCE FICTION, THE SERIES PREDICTED. FROM MODERN-DAY PHONES TO GIANT TV SCREENS, SOME OF THE TECHNOLOGY OF THE FUTURE BEAMING TO THE PRESENT INCLUDE:

Video Conferencing It's hard to imagine now that even twenty years ago, face-to-face video calls seemed unlikely. Some companies had video conferencing, but now, almost any smartphone can host live video chats.

Large-screen Monitors When *Star Trek* debuted in the 1960s, the only screens as big as the one on the bridge were in a movie theater. Now screens that are large enough to fill the bridge of a starship are readily available.

Cell Phones Early cellular flip phones looked so much like TOS communicators that it shouldn't be a surprise that Martin Cooper, who is credited with the development of the first cell phone, cites *Star Trek* as his inspiration.

CAT scans Scientific and medical scanning has come a long way since *Star Trek* debuted. Devices similar to hand-held tricorders that take readings of vital statistics are close to becoming reality, but phone-linked watches are already a step in that direction. The medical beds in sickbay preceded real-life CAT and MRI scanners by only a few years.

Talking Computers AI in computers and phones may be prevalent now, but when *Star Trek: The Next Generation* first aired, the idea of a computer that interacted through voice command was far ahead of its time.

3-D Printer This technology is quite different from a replicator that can instantaneously brew up a hot cup of Earl Grey tea, but it is step in the right direction.

Tablets The Personal Access Display Device (PADD) first shown in *The Next Generation* seemed to belong in the twenty-fourth century with its thin casing and touchscreen interface. Now tablet computers have become a staple of modern life.

Bluetooth Earpiece Lieutenant Uhura's earpiece allowed her mobility while monitoring internal and external communications. Bluetooth headsets now offer the same benefit without having to enroll in Starfleet Academy.

Universal Translator Several phone apps allow for near instantaneous translation among dozens of Earth languages. Sadly, none will work for alien languages … yet.

MY FAVORITE ANDROID

THE CONCEPT OF A ROBOT OR ARTIFICIAL HUMAN EXISTED ALMOST AS SOON AS SCIENCE FICTION WAS BORN. FROM A STORYTELLING PERSPECTIVE, ROBOTS ALLOW CHARACTERS TO GAUGE THEIR OWN HUMANITY AGAINST THAT OF A LIFE-FORM CREATED IN THEIR IMAGE. *STAR TREK* EXPLORED THIS CONCEPT TIME AND AGAIN, SOMETIMES WITH SURPRISING RESULTS.

Ruk Built by the mysterious Old Ones on Exo III, the powerful Ruk helped Dr. Roger Korby create new androids as well as a "perfect" body for Korby's own consciousness. When the Old Ones tried to destroy their creations, Ruk rebelled and killed them.

TOS "WHAT ARE LITTLE GIRLS MADE OF?"

Mudd's Androids Con man Harry Mudd found himself ruling a planet of androids created by the Makers from the Andromeda Galaxy. Mudd had hundreds of beautiful female androids created that served Mudd because he'd given them purpose.

TOS "I, MUDD"

Sargon's Androids Three beings of pure mental force contacted the *Enterprise* crew and asked to inhabit bodies while constructing androids to house their minds. But living in a physical body proved too corrupting for the aliens, and after one died, the others allowed their minds to dissipate before the android bodies could be used.

TOS "RETURN TO TOMORROW"

Rayna Kapec The immortal Flint built Rayna as a companion and tried to stir emotion in her by encouraging an attraction to Kirk. She soon short-circuited, unable to handle the intense emotions of her feelings for both men.

TOS "REQUIEM FOR METHUSALAH"

Exocomps Originally designed to be a mobile tool service mechanism, the exocomps eventually developed sentience, inspiring Data to fight for their rights as free individuals.

TNG "THE QUALITY OF LIFE"

Automated Personnel Unit The Pralor and the Cravics built nearly identical androids to fight their war, but the androids rose up against them when they tried to cease hostilities. Both societies were destroyed and the armies of Automated Personnel Units continued the fighting.

VGR "PROTOTYPE"

Think Tank Intelligence A Delta Quadrant artificial intelligence that had no name, but was described as having the "mind of a mathematician and the soul of an artist."

VGR "THINK TANK"

Data The Starfleet officer was one of only five Soong-type androids. Constructed on Omicron Theta after his brothers B-4 and Lore, Data was deactivated just before the Crystalline Entity attacked the colony. The *U.S.S. Tripoli* found and reactivated Data, and he eventually entered Starfleet Academy and became a valued member of the *Enterprise*-D crew.

TNG

SYSTEM ERROR

Despite advances in artificial intelligence in the twenty-third and twenty-fourth centuries, glitches can still occur and cause life-threatening or even planet-threatening situations. The crews in *Star Trek* often faced computerized intelligences that exceeded their programming. Many times, a good dose of illogic was all it required to stop a computer's murderous rampage.

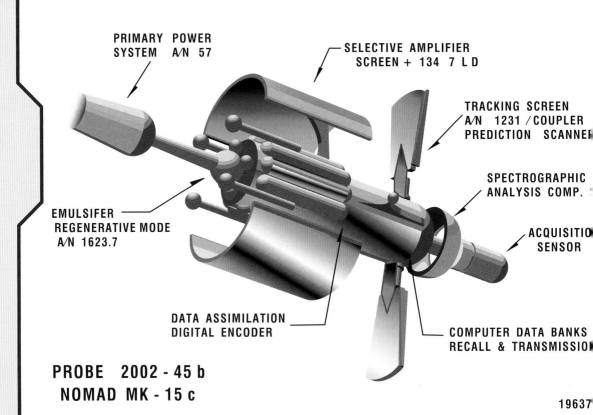

PRIMARY POWER SYSTEM A/N 57

SELECTIVE AMPLIFIER SCREEN + 134 7 L D

TRACKING SCREEN A/N 1231 / COUPLER PREDICTION SCANNER

SPECTROGRAPHIC ANALYSIS COMP.

EMULSIFER REGENERATIVE MODE A/N 1623.7

ACQUISITION SENSOR

DATA ASSIMILATION DIGITAL ENCODER

COMPUTER DATA BANKS RECALL & TRANSMISSION

PROBE 2002 - 45 b
NOMAD MK - 15 c

19637

Nomad An Earth probe merged with an alien probe, Tan Ru, to form an entirely new machine with the faulty programming that decreed it kill anything that was imperfect. After killing four billion Malurians, it mistook Kirk for its creator, and the captain used that confusion to prove Nomad itself was imperfect, causing the probe to self-destruct.

TOS "THE CHANGELING"

Vaal The primitive natives of Gamma Trianguli IV worshiped Vaal as a god. An unknown species built the computer thousands of years earlier, but a massive phaser barrage from the *Enterprise* drained Vaal's power, freeing the natives from its domination.

TOS "THE APPLE"

Shore Leave Planet Computer After its Caretaker died, the computer system on the "Shore Leave" planet became tired of what it saw as a life of servitude and wanted to use the *Enterprise* to escape and seek out its "brother computers." The *Enterprise* crew was able to convince it that men and machines could coexist peacefully.

TAS "ONCE UPON A PLANET"

Enterprise "Joker" After passing through a strange energy field, part of the field cloud entered into the *Enterprise* computer systems. Strange pranks began to occur on the crew until Kirk tricked the computer into returning through an energy field where it was reabsorbed.

TAS "PRACTICAL JOKER"

V'Ger Originally launched from Earth in the twentieth century, the *Voyager* 6 probe eventually crash-landed on a machine planet where the inhabitants rebuilt the damaged probe to fulfill its programming . . . literally. The newly named V'ger traveled the Galaxy "learning all that is learnable" and became self-aware. It needed to join with its creator to finish its mission. With its NASA creators long dead, Commander Will Decker made that sacrifice and joined with V'Ger to save Earth.

STAR TREK: THE MOTION PICTURE

Iconian Probe A computer virus originating in a probe from the ancient Iconian civilization destroyed the *U.S.S. Yamato* before infecting Data, the *Enterprise*-D, and a Romulan. A cold systems reboot was enough to save Data and both ships.

TNG "CONTAGION"

"Pup" After accidentally downloading a playful and puppylike virus into the Deep Space 9 computer system from an alien probe, O'Brien had to create a "doghouse" subroutine to keep it contained.

DS9 "FORSAKEN"

Landru For six thousand years the machine known as Landru ruled the people of the planet Beta III, absorbing the will of the populace into the collective known as the Body. Once a living humanoid, Landru wanted to end his world's warlike ways, and built a machine that he programmed with his identity. When Kirk forced Landru to realize that his plan had become as evil as the wars he sought to prevent, the machine self-destructed.

TOS "RETURN OF THE ARCHONS"

Dreadnought Originally a Cardassian weapon of mass destruction, B'Elanna Torres reprogrammed Dreadnought to attack a Cardassian outpost while she was with the Maquis. Torres was later forced to destroy it after the weapon reappeared in the Delta Quadrant.

VGR "DREADNOUGHT"

Automated Repair Space Station The crew of *Enterprise* NX-01 discovered a highly advanced space station that catered to their needs as it repaired the ship. However, the computerized system used humanoid synaptic pathways for its processing and attempted to fake Mayweather's death to use his mind. The crew appeared to destroy the station, however, it was seen repairing itself.

ENT "DEAD STOP"

M-5 Dr. Richard Daystrom used his memory engrams to create the multitronic computer, but when its self-preservation kicked in during testing it attacked several Starfleet vessels. Kirk confronted the computer with the morality of its actions and it deactivated itself.

TOS "THE ULTIMATE COMPUTER"

THE ORIGINAL SERIES DIDN'T HAVE THE TECHNOLOGY OR BUDGET THAT LATER SHOWS POSSESSED TO CREATE THE COMPUTER-GENERATED BATTLES EXPECTED TODAY, BUT THE PRODUCTION MANAGED TO AMP UP THE TENSION WITH STRATEGIC SCRIPTING (AND OF COURSE, SOME SHAKING SEATS). SOME OF THE MOST FAMOUS STARSHIP BATTLES AND STRATEGIES INCLUDE:

Neutral Zone Engagement When a Romulan bird-of-prey with its cloaking device faced down the *Enterprise* near the Neutral Zone both captains engaged in a game of cat and mouse—pitting the speed and maneuverability of the *Enterprise* against the Romulans' cloak and plasma torpedoes. Kirk critically damaged the bird-of-prey and rather than be taken captive, the Romulan captain destroyed his ship.

TOS "BALANCE OF TERROR"

Battle of the Mutara Nebula When his archenemy Khan commandeered the *U.S.S. Reliant* and crippled the *Enterprise*, Kirk retreated into the Mutara Nebula, which effectively disabled both ships' shields and sensors. The captain took tactical advantage of Khan's two-dimensional thinking. Sinking below the horizontal level in which the ships had been fighting, the *Enterprise* managed to deliver killing blows before Khan activated the Genesis torpedo, destroying *Reliant* and the nebula.

STAR TREK II: THE WRATH OF KHAN

Battle of Wolf 359 The engagement with the Borg at Wolf 359 went down as one of the Federation's worst defeats. A Borg cube carrying the assimilated Captain Picard, with his knowledge of Starfleet strengths and tactics, helped the Borg destroy almost all forty ships in the fleet assembled to battle the cube. Over eleven thousand lives were lost, including Benjamin Sisko's wife, Jennifer.

TNG "THE BEST OF BOTH WORLDS"/
DS9 "EMISSARY"

The Corbomite Maneuver Kirk claimed all Starfleet ships contain "corbomite," a substance that creates a reactive, destructive force against any attacker as a bluff when dealing with a captain in the First Federation.

TOS "THE CORBOMITE MANEUVER"

Battle of Khitomer As the *Enterprise*-A traveled to Khitomer to prevent conspirators from stopping the scheduled peace conference, General Chang attacked in a cloaked Klingon vessel. Even with the aid of Captain Sulu and the *U.S.S. Excelsior*, Chang's ship continued to have the upper hand until Spock realized that cloaked ships still vent plasma exhaust. Uhura suggested using their equipment for cataloging gaseous anomalies to find the cloaked ship. A modified torpedo helped the Federation ships target and destroy Chang's vessel.

STAR TREK VI: THE UNDISCOVERED COUNTRY

Operation: Return After Captain Sisko convinced Starfleet Command that the Bajoran Wormhole was the key to protecting the Alpha Quadrant, he led the fleet to retake Deep Space 9. Sisko baited Gul Dukat's forces, trying to open a hole in their defenses, and Dukat countered by breaking off some fighters in a move that was a clear trap. Starfleet forces were close to defeat when the Klingon Defense Force arrived to render aid. Though the minefield that had prevented additional Dominion forces from coming through the wormhole was destroyed, Sisko convinced the wormhole aliens to make the incoming Dominion warships disappear.

DS9 "FAVOR THE BOLD"

Battle of Maxia (The Picard Maneuver) When Picard was captain of the *U.S.S. Stargazer*, the ship was attacked and damaged by what was later found to be a Ferengi vessel. Picard ordered the *Stargazer* to go to high warp for a millisecond, confusing the Ferengi into seeing the ship in two places at once. The Stargazer was able to destroy the Ferengi ship and the tactic became known as the "Picard Maneuver."

TNG "THE BATTLE"

First Battle of Chin'toka The allied Federation and Klingon forces were joined by the Romulan Star Empire to attack the *Chin'toka* system, which looked relatively undefended. An orbital weapons platform caused difficulty, until Chief O'Brien came up with a way to trick the platform into destroying its own power source, leading to an allied victory.

DS9 "TEARS OF THE PROPHETS"

Riker Maneuver While fighting the Son'a, Riker ordered the Bussard collector to gather the unstable matron gas present in the Briar Patch. Steering precisely, he released the clouds of gas between the attackers and the *Enterprise*. When the Son'a fired, the gas ignited, destroying one of their own ships. La Forge jokingly dubbed this the "Riker Maneuver."

STAR TREK: INSURRECTION

"Year of Hell" Janeway and *Voyager* were on their last legs after a year of evading Annorax and his temporal warship. The captain led a small coalition of ships, with inside help from Paris and Chakotay who were trapped on Annorax's vessel. The allies proved no match for the timeship, forcing Janeway to ram the damaged *Voyager* into the temporal core of the timeship, destroying it and resetting the correct timeline.

VGR "YEAR OF HELL"

Battle of Azati Prime Xindi-reptillian commander Dolim and three other ships attacked and severely damaged *Enterprise* NX-01. The Starfleet crew managed to take out one ship before they were about to be destroyed, until Xindi scientist Degra ordered Dolim to call off the attack.

ENT "AZATI PRIME"

The Picard Maneuver

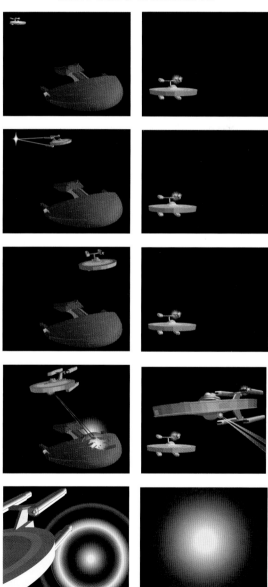

▲ Actual Location   ▲ Sensor Readings

DRESS CODE

THESE ARE JUST SOME OF THE MORE POPULAR LOOKS THAT STARFLEET CREWS HAVE MODELED OVER THE CENTURIES:

Twenty-second-century jumpsuits

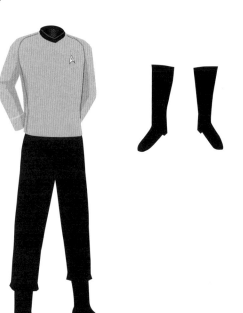

Twenty-third-century duty uniforms

Late twenty-third-century duty uniforms

Twenty-fourth-century jumpsuits

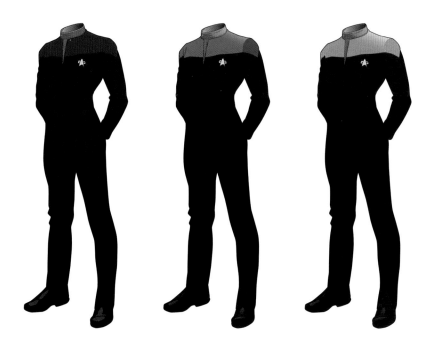

Voyager-era jumpsuits

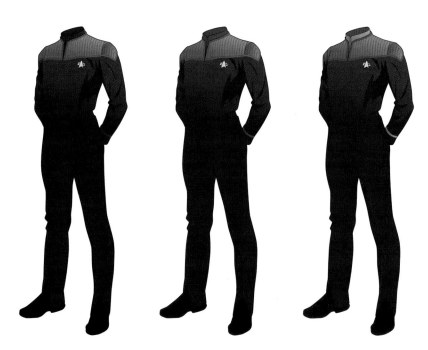

Dominion War-era duty uniforms

Kelvin Timeline duty uniforms

Twenty-third-century dress uniform

Twenty-fourth-century dress uniforms

If you ever noticed that things happened in 47s in the various *Star Trek* series, you're not imagining things. Staff Writer Joe Menosky gets the credit for the 47 fever that ran through the shows of the twenty-fourth century. He graduated from Pomona College, where the college was home to a professor who claimed (as a joke) to have devised a mathematical proof that all numbers are equal to 47. Provable or not, the other writers began to pepper the number almost everywhere, in a fad that spread across genre television and film, ultimately affecting J. J. Abrams long before he took the reins on the franchise.

1. Code 47 means "captain's eyes only." TNG "Conspiracy"

2. Vintage of wine is 2247. TNG "Family"

3. 47 million strands of energy are within the nebula. TNG "Imaginary Friend"

4. 47 sentry pods guard the Lysian Central Command. TNG "Conundrum"

5. The Cliffs of Heaven are holodeck program 47-C. TNG "Conundrum"

6. Spot eats Feline Supplement 47. TNG "Data's Day"

7. Ogawa was on level 47 of the Ktarian game. TNG "The Game"

8. Temperature in reaction chamber has increased by 47 percent. TNG "True Q"

9. Riker is held in ward 47. TNG "Frame of Mind"

10. The *Enterprise*-D has to leave 47 people behind. TNG "Descent"

11. Starbase 47 is mentioned. TNG "Parallels"

12. 47 instances of Darmok in the computer. TNG "Darmok"

13. The probe will overload the shields in 47 seconds. TNG "Nth Degree"

14. Authorization code is alpha-4-7. TNG "Genesis"

15. Subroutine C-47 is affected in the computer. TNG "A Fistful of Datas"

16. A poem Data reads has a 47 minute period of silence. TNG "Interface"

17. Power levels drop by 47 percent. TNG "Emergence"

18. Riker is the commanding officer of Starbase 247. TNG "All Good Things …"

19. **Runabout *Rio Grande* shows a button labeled 47. DS9 "Emissary"**

20. **47 people on the moon left willingly. DS9 "Progress"**

21. **Rule of Acquisition #47: "Don't trust a man wearing a better suit than your own." DS9 "Rivals"**

22. **Dax changes course to 130 mark 47. DS9 "Playing God"**

23. **Kira's access code is 5-4-7. DS9 "Defiant"**

24. **Cardassian outpost 47 is mentioned. DS9 "Defiant"**

25. **Red Squad was Cadet Training Squad 47. DS9 "Homefront"/"Paradise Lost"**

26. **Romulans' quarters are moved to section 47. DS9 "Visionary"**

27. **O'Brien is about to win his 47th dart game. DS9 "Shakaar"**

28. **47 people are aboard the *Defiant*. DS9 "The Adversary"**

29. **Weapons locker is number 47. DS9 "Hard Time"**

30. **The Dominion battleship moves at warp 4.7. DS9 "Valiant"**

31. **Kasidy Yates's baseball uniform number is 47. DS9 "Take Me out to the Holosuite"**

32. **Ezri needs to eliminate 47 of the 48 Vulcans on the station as suspects. DS9 "Field of Fire"**

33. **The Doctor is programmed with the experiences from 47 medical officers. VGR "Parallax"**

34. **Blood-gas infuser can only keep Neelix alive 47 more minutes. VGR "Phage"**

35. **47 bioneural gel packs are in storage. VGR "Learning Curve"**

36. **Janeway's program is saved in memory block 47-alpha. VGR "Projections"**

37. **Harry Kim's office is level six, subsection 47. VGR "Non Sequitur"**

38. **Tanis says it will take Suspiria 47 hours to respond. VGR "Cold Fire"**

39. **Torres remodulates the frequency five times on 47 frequencies. VGR "Deadlock"**

40. **Humans share 47 genetic markers with the Voth. VGR "Distant Origins"**

41. **Part of the episode takes place on Day 47. VGR "The Year of Hell, Part I"**

42. **Voyager can access 47 million channels simultaneously. VGR "Concerning Flight"**

43. **Seven of Nine gauges there are 47 Borg ships in the nebula. VGR "Endgame"**

44. **47 El-Aurian refugees are saved by the *U.S.S. Enterprise*-B. *Star Trek Generations***

45. **Picard's security clearance is "Picard four-seven-alpha-tango." *Star Trek: First Contact***

46. **In the *Kelvin* Timeline, 47 Klingon warbirds are lost to Nero. *Star Trek* (2009)**

47. **And perhaps time travel can account for this one occurring in The Original Series: the *SS Beagle* had 47 crew members. "Bread and Circuses"**

SIGNS AND SYMBOLS

The Galaxy is a big place and not everything is labeled. Luckily for Starfleet personnel, most of the major spacefaring races have unique signs and symbols that let you know who they are . . . and if you should be afraid.

U.S.S. Enterprise Command Insignia

United Federation of Planets Flag

Starfleet Academy Logo

United Federation of Planets Emblem

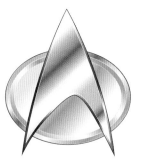

Twenty-fourth century Starfleet Insignia

Starfleet Command Logo

Vulcan IDIC

Emblem of the Klingon Empire

Symbol of the Bajoran Faith

Emblem of the Romulan Star Empire

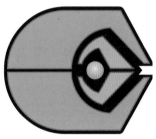

Seal of the Ferengi Alliance

Symbol of the Cardassian Union

Symbol of the Dominion

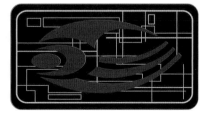

Symbol of the Borg

Chapter 4

THE FINAL FRONTIER

A History of the Future

HISTORICAL FIGURE CAMEOS

BETWEEN TIME TRAVEL, HOLOGRAPHIC REPRESENTATIONS, AND NEAR-IMMORTAL BEINGS, OFFICERS IN STARFLEET HAVE HAD THE OPPORTUNITY TO MEET A WIDE RANGE OF HISTORICAL FIGURES.

Amelia Earhart Captain Janeway got to meet one of her inspirations when the *Voyager* crew discovered the missing pilot in suspended animation in the Delta Quadrant.

VGR "THE 37'S"

Doc Holliday and Virgil, Morgan, and Wyatt Earp The Melkotians created replicas of the gunslingers to recreate the famous Gunfight at the OK Corral, with Kirk and his crew on the losing side.

TOS "SPECTRE OF THE GUN"

Sigmund Freud Data's nightmares led him to a holographic therapy session with the famous psychologist. Ultimately, the *Enterprise*-D's actual counselor, Deanna Troi, was able to help him.

TNG "PHANTASMS"

Socrates, Lord Byron, and Mahatma Gandhi If a hologram wants to learn to be Human, he could do far worse than these three historical figures. The Doctor added their behaviors to his own subroutines. However, the darker side of each man's personality began to turn the Doctor into a dark version of himself.

VGR "DARKLING"

Samuel Clemens/Jack London The crew of the *Enterprise*-D traveled to San Francisco in the nineteenth century and met the two famous authors. They also met a younger version of their long-lived bartender, Guinan. While Clemens was already established as a famed humorist, London was still a bellboy.

TNG "TIME'S ARROW"

Abraham Lincoln and Genghis Khan Kirk couldn't believe a floating Abraham Lincoln in space was really the esteemed president—and it wasn't. The replica, created to help Excalbians understand the Human concepts of good and evil, acted like the real Honest Abe, while replicas of Genghis Khan and other historical figures stayed in character as well.

TOS "THE SAVAGE CURTAIN"

Leonardo da Vinci When the immortal Flint met Captain Kirk, he claimed to have been a number of figures throughout Earth history, including Solomon, Alexander the Great, and Brahms. He also claimed to be da Vinci. Captain Janeway might have a better idea of the truth. She created a holodeck version of the maestro for inspiration during her long voyage through the Delta Quadrant.

TOS "REQUIEM FOR METHUSELAH"/
VGR "SCORPION"

Albert Einstein, Stephen Hawking, and Isaac Newton Data recreated three of the greatest scientists in Human history on the holodeck to observe them in a poker game, with the actual Stephen Hawking playing himself—the only person in *Star Trek* history to do so. Years later, Q brought the real Sir Isaac Newton to *Voyager* to weigh in on Quinn's death wish.

TNG "DESCENT"/
VGR "DEATH WISH"

FROM QUARKS TO QUARK'S

SOME OF THE SCIENTIFIC TERMS USED IN *STAR TREK* COME FROM THE MINDS OF THE WRITERS TO EXPLAIN HOW IMPOSSIBLE THINGS LIKE TRANSPORTERS, PHASERS AND ANNULAR CONFINEMENT BEAMS CAN WORK. OTHER JARGON BORROWS FROM EXISTING SCIENTIFIC TERMS TO GROUND THE TECHNOBABBLE, BUT IS STILL ULTIMATELY MEANINGLESS IN THE FUTURISTIC CONTEXT. BUT *STAR TREK*, LIKE ALL GOOD SCIENCE FICTION, HAS ALSO RELIED HEAVILY ON REAL PRACTICAL AND THEORETICAL SCIENCE TO GROUND MANY OF ITS MEMORABLE STORIES IN FACT.

Neutrinos Electrically neutral elementary particles. In *Star Trek* they can do many things, including help detect antimatter reactors.

ENT "CIVILIZATION"

Accretion Disk Material in orbit around a massive object like a star or black hole. Flying through one could make your runabout shrink.

DS9 "ONE LITTLE SHIP"

Black Hole The remains of a collapsed star. Flying through one could send you through space or time or just make you feel like you had.

STAR TREK: THE MOTION PICTURE / STAR TREK (2009)

Plasma An ionized state of gas (in physics). Electro-plasma systems aboard a starship are the primary form of energy distribution. Some species also use plasma-based weaponry.

ENT "SHADOWS OF P'JEM"

Photons Elementary particles of light. They can be used for torpedo-like weapons as well as holograms and there are even some photonic life-forms.

STAR TREK: THE MOTION PICTURE /
VGR "BRIDE OF CHAOTICA!"

Quark An elementary particle that makes up matter . . . whereas Quark is an elementary part of Deep Space 9 that serves drinks and makes profits.

DS9 "EMISSARY"

Protons Subatomic particles that have a positive electrical charge. They can also be used as beam weapons or bursts to help compensate for antimatter drains.

VGR "NIGHT"/ "DEADLOCK"

Wormhole Theoretical tunnel through the fabric of space and time. Natural ones were found to be unstable, and the only artificial one known is the Bajoran wormhole.

DS9 "EMISSARY"

Dark Matter Theoretical substance that may make up twenty-seven percent of the universe. It does not interact with electromagnetic rays, which is how it gets its name. It also can hide unfriendly life-forms.

VGR "GOOD SHEPHERD"

Antimatter Unlike dark matter, antimatter is real, but only at a subatomic level. While matter and antimatter will create an explosive discharge when they meet, so far, all the antimatter in the world would barely generate even a small amount of power.

TOS "OBSESSION"

Gamma Rays This electromagnetic radiation occurs when atomic nuclei decay and ionize other atoms, which can cause biological damage. In *Star Trek*, gamma radiation had a number of uses, including recrystallizing dilithium and leaving a detectable trace from Borg weapons.

VGR "CHILD'S PLAY"/
STAR TREK IV: THE VOYAGE HOME

RETRO-FASHION FORWARD

Clothing designers aspire to be fashion forward, but it's a challenge to design for trends three centuries in advance. Original *Star Trek* costumer William Ware Theiss claimed in the book *The Making of Star Trek* that "the degree to which a costume is considered sexy is directly proportional to how accident-prone it appears to be." That theory was proven true on The Original Series with some of the most stunning (and often outlandish) alien outfits ever created.

Eve, Magda, and Ruth "Mudd's Women"

Andrea "What Are Little Girls Made Of?"

Show girls "Shore Leave"

Sylvia "Catspaw"

Capellan warriors "Friday's Child"

Apollo and Lieutenant Palamas "Who Mourns for Adonais?"

Tamoon and Shahna "The Gamesters of Triskelion"

Flint and Rayna Kapec "Requiem for Methuselah"

Deela "Wink of an Eye"

Dr. Sevrin's group "The Way to Eden"

LIST #52 TO B-4 OR NOT TO B-4 . . .

"All the world's a stage,
And all the men and women merely players . . . "

THE BARD'S IMMORTAL WORDS COULD NOT BE TRUER. *STAR TREK*
AND SHAKESPEARE HAVE A LONG HISTORY TOGETHER, EVEN BEFORE
NOTED SHAKESPEAREAN ACTOR PATRICK STEWART SIGNED ON TO PLAY
CAPTAIN JEAN-LUC PICARD. OVER THE YEARS ALL THE INCARNATIONS OF
STAR TREK HAVE REFERENCED THE FAMED PLAYWRIGHT.

"The Conscience of the King"
The Karidian Company of Players performed *Hamlet* and *Macbeth for Enterprise* personnel. . . . . TOS

"Plato's Stepchildren"
Kirk recited a sonnet while under the Platonians' control. . . . . TOS

"Whom Gods Destroy"
Marta claimed she wrote Sonnet 18 "yesterday, as a matter of fact." . . . . TOS

"The Naked Now"
Data paraphrased the famous line with "When you prick me, do I not leak?" . . . . TNG

"Hide and Q"
Q paraphrased and said, "All the galaxy's a stage." . . . . TNG

"Ménage à Troi"
Picard "fought" for Lwaxana Troi with sonnets. . . . . TNG

"Time's Arrow"
Picard and the crew rehearsed scenes from *A Midsummer Night's Dream*. . . . . TNG

"Tapestry"
Q quoted *Hamlet* to Picard. . . . . TNG

"Emergence"
Data performed the final scene from *The Tempest*. . . . . TNG

"Inter Arma Enim Silent Leges"
Section 31's Luther Sloan explained that the phrase "Never say die" originated from
The Merchant of Venice. DS9

"Tuvix"
Tuvix lifted from Shylock's speech in *The Merchant of Venice* to justify his existence. . . . . VGR

Star Trek IV: The Voyage Home
McCoy quoted "Angels and ministers of grace, defend us," from *Hamlet*.

Shakespeare's words provided a number of episode titles as well . . .

"Dagger of the Mind"
(TOS) *Macbeth*

"The Conscience of the King"
(TOS) *Hamlet*

"By Any Other Name"
(TOS) *Romeo and Juliet*

"All Our Yesterdays"
(TOS) *Macbeth*

"How Sharper Than a Serpent's Tooth"
(TAS) *King Lear*

"Thine Own Self"
(TNG) *Hamlet*

"Past Prologue"
(DS9) The Tempest

"Once More unto the Breach"
(DS9) *Henry V*

"Dogs of War"
(DS9) *Julius Caesar*

"Mortal Coil"
(VGR) *Hamlet*

Star Trek VI: The Undiscovered Country
Hamlet

TREKLIT

STAR TREK SET THE TONE OF EXPLORING MORALITY AND FORCING PEOPLE TO THINK ABOUT THE TURBULENT 1960S WITH ALLEGORIES FOR RACISM, WAR, AND CIVIL RIGHTS. PEPPERED THROUGHOUT THE WRITING WERE QUOTES AND ALLUSIONS TO MANY LITERARY REFERENCES. AS THE PHENOMENON GREW TO FILMS AND SEQUEL SERIES, ALL OF THE STAR TREK SERIES DREW ON THE VAST CLASSIC LITERATURE OF EARTH TO LET CHARACTERS MAKE THEIR POINT.

"Tyger Tyger, burning bright"/"Once upon a midnight dreary" While under Charlie Evans's mental control, Spock recited William Blake's "The Tyger" and Edgar Allen Poe's "The Raven."

TOS "CHARLIE X"

Les Misérables Michael Eddington likened Sisko's pursuit of him for leaving Starfleet to join the Maquis as being similar to Victor Hugo's character Inspector Javert's obsession with Jean Valjean.

DS9 "FOR THE UNIFORM"

Ulysses Captain Picard took the James Joyce classic to read when he vacationed on Risa, while Malcom Reed brought it along during Shuttlepod One's trip back to *Enterprise* NX-01.

TNG "CAPTAIN'S HOLIDAY"/
ENT "SHUTTLEPOD ONE"

Moby Dick Khan paraphrased lines from Herman Melville's classic novel of revenge as he prepared to activate the Genesis torpedo before he died. Lily Sloane compared Picard's quest to kill the Borg to Ahab's obsession with Moby Dick.

STAR TREK II: THE WRATH OF KHAN/
STAR TREK: FIRST CONTACT

Peter Pan As his final command before the *Enterprise*-A was to be decommissioned, Captain Kirk ordered the course heading: "Second star to the right. And straight on 'til morning," from the children's play by J.M. Barrie.

STAR TREK VI: THE UNDISCOVERED COUNTRY

A Tale of Two Cities Spock gave Kirk a birthday gift of Charles Dickens's classic, which prompted Kirk to read the famous opening lines: "It was the best of times, it was the worst of times." Later, after Spock died, Kirk quoted the last lines of the novel "It is a far, far better thing that I do, than I have ever done; it is a far, far better rest that I go to than I have ever known." In *Deep Space Nine*, Ezri Dax once loaned Julian Bashir a copy of the book as well.

STAR TREK II: THE WRATH OF KHAN/
DS9 "EXTREME MEASURES"

Bible The ambassadorial conference on Babel was a reference to the biblical tower where humanity began speaking different languages. The immortal Flint claimed to be Lazarus as well as Methuselah. Spock compared tribbles to the "lilies of the valley," from Matthew 8:26. The episode title "And the Children Shall Lead" is paraphrased from Isaiah 11:6. Dr. McCoy compared the Genesis Device (itself a reference to the book of Genesis) to being able to make a planet in six minutes instead of six days.

TOS "REQUIEM FOR METHUSELAH/
"AND THE CHILDREN SHALL LEAD"/
STAR TREK: THE WRATH OF KHAN

"It is better to rule in Hell than to serve in Heaven." Kirk explained Khan's reference to John Milton's poem about humanity's expulsion from Eden when the evil augment was exiled to Ceti Alpha V.

TOS "SPACE SEED"

Sherlock Holmes Spock quoted the famous line from Sir Arthur Conan Doyle's detective: "If you eliminate the impossible, whatever remains, however improbable, must be the truth." Data often played Sherlock Holmes in the holodeck, with Geordi as Watson.

STAR TREK VI: THE UNDISCOVERED COUNTRY/ TNG "ELEMENTARY, DEAR DATA"

Mark Twain Not only did the *Enterprise*-D crew meet the famous author (as well as Jack London) when they traveled back in time, Picard, Kasidy Yates, and the Doctor have all paraphrased Twain's famous quote, "Reports of my death have been greatly exaggerated."

TNG "TIME'S ARROW"/"SAMARITAN SNARE"/ DS9 "WHAT YOU LEAVE BEHIND"/ VGR "BODY AND SOUL"

Beowulf Harry Kim played the hero of the epic poem in the holodeck when a photonic being became trapped in the holodeck and took on the role of the monstrous Grendel.

VGR "HEROES AND DEMONS"

Alice's Adventures in Wonderland/Through the Looking Glass On the Shore Leave planet, McCoy followed a white rabbit from Lewis Carroll's *Alice's Adventures in Wonderland* while later the Platonians' made Kirk and Spock sing a song about Tweedledee and Tweedledum and other Lewis Carroll references like "mimsy" and "borogroves." The *Deep Space Nine* episode "Through the Looking Glass" title came from the Carroll books as well.

TOS "SHORE LEAVE"/"PLATO'S STEPCHILDREN"/ DS9 "THROUGH THE LOOKING GLASS"

HISTORY IN THE MAKING

Many times Starfleet crew members have traveled back in time, and even been part of history. Some of the most memorable eras visited have been:

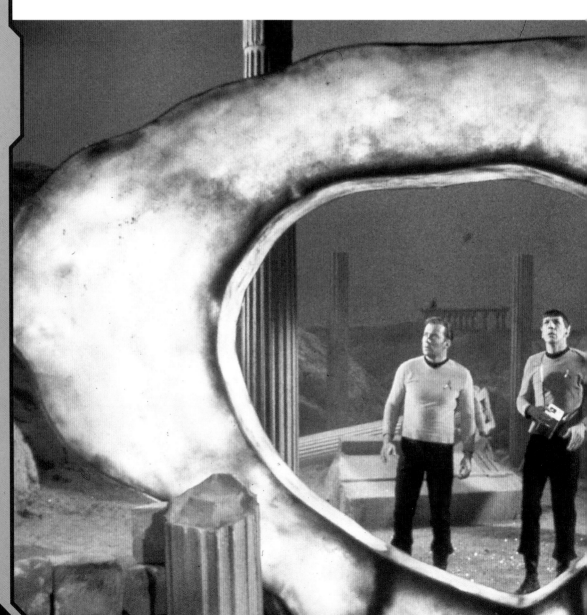

Earth, 3.5 billion years ago After bouncing Picard around in time, Q took the captain back billions of years to the very moment that proteins should have formed the first life on Earth.

TNG "ALL GOOD THINGS . . ."

8877 Vulcan Spock journeyed to his home city ShiKahr in the Vulcan year 8877.

TAS "YESTERYEAR"

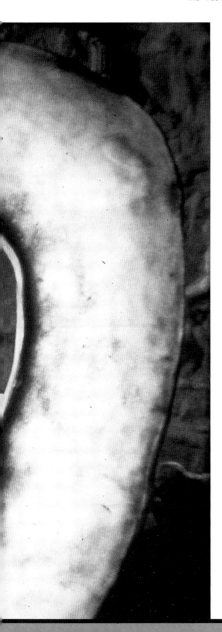

Nineteenth-Century San Francisco Picard and most of his senior staff traveled back in time to rescue Data.

TNG "TIME'S ARROW"

1930s New York McCoy, Kirk, and Spock traveled to this time and place to undo history and then fix it.

TOS "THE CITY ON THE EDGE OF FOREVER"

1944 The crew of *Enterprise* NX-01 traveled back to a 1944 where the Temporal Cold War changed history so that the Nazis had won World War II.

ENT "STORM FRONT"

1947 Roswell, New Mexico Quark, Rom, and Nog accidentally jumped back to 1947 to cause the famed Roswell Incident.

DS9 "LITTLE GREEN MEN"

1950s New York Benjamin Sisko lived an alternate version of himself and the DS9 crew in Earth's less enlightened past.

DS9 "FAR BEYOND THE STARS"

1960s Earth On more than one occasion, the *U.S.S. Enterprise* traveled back to the time in which the series was filmed.

TOS "TOMORROW IS YESTERDAY"/"ASSIGNMENT: EARTH"

1986 San Francisco The *Enterprise* bridge crew took a Klingon ship back in time to retrieve a pair of extinct whales to avert a future disaster.

STAR TREK IV: THE VOYAGE HOME

1996 Los Angeles The *U.S.S. Voyager* crew traveled back in time to stop the future from impacting the past.

VGR "FUTURE'S END"

Stardate 4523.7 The Deep Space 9 ops crew traveled back to Deep Space Station K-7 to interact with Captain Kirk's crew on the original *U.S.S. Enterprise*.

DS9 "TRIALS AND TRIBBLE-ATIONS"

Sarpeidon's past While on the planet Sarpeidon, Spock and McCoy visited its ice age while Kirk spent time in its Elizabethan-like age.

TOS "ALL OUR YESTERDAYS"

IMMINENT EVENTS

WHILE PEOPLE LIKE TO BELIEVE THE FUTURE IS UNWRITTEN, FROM THE PERSPECTIVE OF THE FUTURE ACCORDING TO *STAR TREK*, IT'S ALREADY SET IN STONE. SOME OF THE HISTORICAL EVENTS THE SERIES HAS LOOKED FORWARD TO INCLUDE:

Twentieth Century

1992-1996 The cataclysmic Eugenics Wars occur. Genetically augmented "supermen," including the warlord Khan Noonien Singh, will take control of most of Earth during this period, at least from a 1960s perspective.

TOS "SPACE SEED"/ENT "THE AUGMENTS"

Twenty-first Century

2024 The government-created Sanctuary Districts that are supposed to help deal with poverty and homelessness will instead lead to worsening conditions for the population. Gabriel Bell will help reform the system after the riots that bear his name.

DS9 "PAST TENSE"

2026-2053 Over 600 million people will die during the third world war that starts around 2026, with Colonel Phillip Green's eco-terrorists alone killing some thirty-seven million people. A cease-fire will be negotiated in 2053.

TOS "THE SAVAGE CURTAIN"/
STAR TREK: FIRST CONTACT

2063 Zefram Cochrane's first warp-capable ship, the *Phoenix*, launches on April 5, 2063. It will attract the attention of a Vulcan ship and bring about Earth's first official contact with another race.

STAR TREK: FIRST CONTACT

2067 The United Earth Space Probe Agency launches the Friendship 1 probe to find intelligent species in the Galaxy.

VGR "FRIENDSHIP ONE"

Unknown date Humpback whales become extinct.

Twenty-second Century

2103 Jean-Luc Picard's ancestors will be among the first settlers on the Martian colonies established in this year.

VGR "LIFESIGNS"

2150 The United Earth government forms.

TNG "ATTACHED"

2151 Earth's first warp 5-capable vessel, *Enterprise* NX-01, launches, expanding humanity's reach into the stars.

ENT "BROKEN BOW"

2153 Xindi attack Earth, destroying parts of Florida, Cuba, and Venezuela.

ENT "THE EXPANSE"

2161 Four species—Humans, Vulcans, Andorians, and Tellarites—form a coalition that will become the United Federation of Planets.

ENT "THESE ARE THE VOYAGES . . ."

2184-2192 Captain Jonathan Archer serves as president of the United Federation of Planets.

ENT "IN A MIRROR, DARKLY"

Twenty-third Century

2245 The *U.S.S. Enterprise* NCC-1701 launches.

TAS "THE COUNTER-CLOCK INCIDENT"

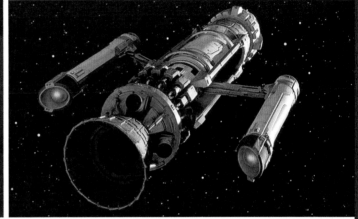

LIST #56 / I COME FROM THE FUTURE

THE TEMPORAL PRIME DIRECTIVE FORBIDS STARFLEET PERSONNEL FROM
CONTAMINATING THE TIMELINE OR PROVIDING INFORMATION TO ANYONE
IN THE PAST THAT COULD CAUSE PARADOXES OR ALTER THE TIMELINES.
BUT MUCH LIKE THE PRIME DIRECTIVE OF NONINTERFERENCE IN PRIMITIVE
CULTURES, SOME OF THESE TEMPORAL RULES ARE BENT FROM TIME TO
TIME. THESE ARE JUST A FEW OF THOSE TIMES . . .

"Yesterday's *Enterprise*" After the *Enterprise*-C came forward from the past, the surviving members of the crew had to return to certain death in order to create a better future.

TNG

"Captain's Holiday" Scientist Kal Dano and two Vorgon thieves traveled from the twenty-seventh century to hide and then steal the powerful Tox Uthat.

TNG

"Time's Arrow" Natives of Devidia II, humanoid shape-shifters, traveled back in time to nineteenth-century Earth to feed on Humans' neural energy until the crew of the *Enterprise*-D could stop them.

TNG

"Firstborn" Alexander Rozhenko went back in time to convince his younger self to follow a warrior's path in order to save Worf's life.

TNG

"One" The Doctor's mobile emitter was a piece of twenty-ninth-century technology he acquired during the encounter with Captain Braxton. When he and Seven had to undergo an emergency beam-out, her Borg nanoprobes merged with his emitter and created an advanced twenty-ninth-century Borg drone. It took the designation "One," and eventually sacrificed itself to keep its unique properties out of the hands of the twenty-fourth-century Borg.

VGR "DRONE"

"Future's End" Captain Braxton of the Federation timeship *Aeon* attacked *Voyager*, claiming that the crew was responsible for the destruction of Earth's solar system in the twenty-ninth century. Both ships were hurled back to 1996 Earth, where they managed to avoid the events that caused the destruction of the Sol system.

VGR

"A Matter of Time" Historian Berlinghoff Rasmussen appeared out of a space-time distortion near Penthara IV. He claimed to be from the twenty-sixth century, but in fact, he was from the twenty-second century and had stolen the time-travel pod from an actual visitor from the future.

TNG

"Relativity" Captain Braxton lived in the late twentieth century for thirty years before *Voyager* arrived, which impacted his mental stability. Rehabilitation in his own time helped him return to duty on a new ship, the *U.S.S. Relativity*. However, a future version of himself suffered from temporal psychosis and tried to come back in time and destroy *Voyager* again.

VGR

"Cold Front" Crewman Daniels didn't appear special until the Suliban, Silik, came on board *Enterprise*. Daniels revealed himself to be a temporal agent and part of one of the factions in the Temporal Cold War in which the *Enterprise* crew found themselves pawns. Daniels would return several times as an agent of that war.

ENT

LIST #57 / TEMPORAL ANOMALIES

As Captain Janeway once said, "I swore I'd never let myself get caught in one of these godforsaken paradoxes—the future is the past, the past is the future, it all gives me a headache." These are just some of the interesting effects temporal anomalies had on Starfleet crews:

Manheim Effect Dr. Paul Manheim created a temporal distortion window where a moment of time repeated itself.

TNG "WE'LL ALWAYS HAVE PARIS"

Energy vortex entity The vortex destroyed the *Enterprise*-D while Picard tried to draw its attention from a shuttlecraft. Picard was thrown backward six hours, where he had the chance to change what happened.

TNG "TIME SQUARED"

Kerr loop A temporal rift was created by intense weaponry discharge near superstring material during the *Enterprise*-C crew's battle with four Romulan warbirds

TNG "YESTERDAY'S *ENTERPRISE*"

Temporal aperture The crew of the *Enterprise*-D discovered a breach inside the quantum singularity engine of a Romulan warbird that formed temporal fragments reducing or accelerating the flow of space-time within them.

TNG "TIMESCAPE"

Anti-time A collision of time and anti-time caused a rupture that spread backward through time until it prevented the beginnings of life on Earth.

TNG "ALL GOOD THINGS . . ."

Gaia barrier The crew of the *Defiant* met their descendants on a planet with a strange energy barrier that was two hundred years out of time.

DS9 "CHILDREN OF TIME"

Dormant chroniton radiation This radiation caused Kes to leap backward throughout her life.

VGR "BEFORE AND AFTER"

Metreon radiation barrier The *Defiant* came to the rescue of a now deceased Starfleet captain whose distress call had been time-shifted three years into the future due to the energy barrier around the planet.

DS9 "THE SOUND OF HER VOICE"

Micro-wormhole The *Voyager* crew established communications with the captain of a Romulan ship in the Alpha Quadrant through a micro-wormhole, only to discover the wormhole sent their message to the past and their potential savior died four years before their mission began.

VGR "EYE OF THE NEEDLE"

Temporal flux distortion The *U.S.S. Bozeman* broke free of a temporal flux distortion it was trapped in for decades and destroyed the *Enterprise*-D. The temporal anomaly then caused the event to occur again and again until Data provided a valuable clue for how to break the loop.

TNG "CAUSE AND EFFECT"

Borg temporal transmitter An older Chakotay and Harry Kim violated the Temporal Prime Directive using a Borg temporal transmitter to save *Voyager* from a disastrous attempt at getting back to the Alpha Quadrant.

VGR "TIMELESS"

Golana portal A time portal sent Molly O'Brien into the distant past, briefly returning her as a young woman until she could be exchanged for her younger self.

DS9 "TIME'S ORPHAN"

Spatial rift This anomaly split the decks of *Voyager* into different timeframes.

VGR "SHATTERED"

Xindi subspace corridor *Enterprise* NX-01 encountered a version of itself thrown into the future, and the crew met their descendants.

ENT "E2"

Black hole When the Romulan mining ship *Narada* and Ambassador Spock's vessel were pulled into a black hole, the event created an alternate reality where Captain Kirk and the *Enterprise* crew had different adventures. The new universe of experiences it created would become known as the *Kelvin* Timeline.

STAR TREK (2009)

Chapter 5

STORIES FROM THE FUTURE

AUTHOR, AUTHOR

STAR TREK EARNED ITS PEDIGREE AS HIGH-QUALITY SCIENCE FICTION RIGHT FROM THE START WHEN GENE RODDENBERRY HIRED NOTED SCIENCE-FICTION AUTHORS TO WRITE FOR THE SHOW. OTHER GENRE FICTION WRITERS ALSO ADDED TO *STAR TREK*, AND WHEN *THE NEXT GENERATION* BEGAN, A YOUNG-ADULT AUTHOR AND FAN WROTE AN EPISODE. SOME OF THE AUTHORS WHO CONTRIBUTED TO BUILDING THE BUDDING PHENOMENON INCLUDE:

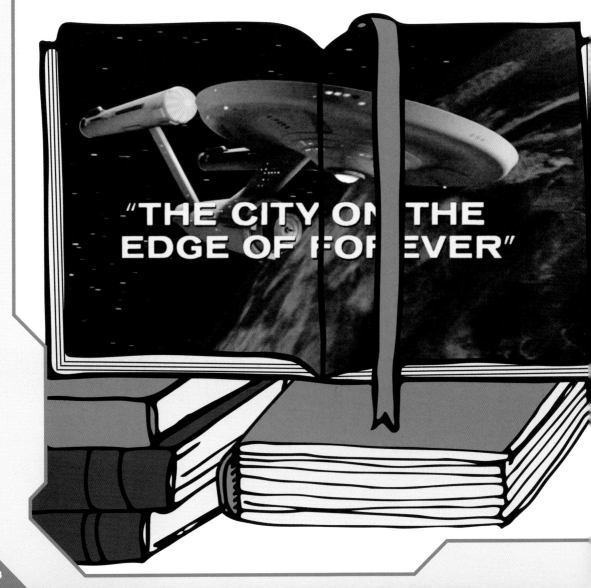

Samuel A. Peeples The novelist known for Westerns was also a fan of science fiction. He wrote The Original Series episode "Where No Man Has Gone Before" and "Beyond the Farthest Star" for *The Animated Series*.

Shari Lewis Best known as the voice and hand behind beloved children's puppet Lamb Chop, Lewis wrote children's books as well as the TOS episode "The Lights of Zetar" with her husband.

Diane Duane The young-adult author—as well as the writer of numerous *Star Trek* books—helped rewrite the script for "Where No One Has Gone Before" for *The Next Generation*.

Harlan Ellison The legendary sci-fi author wrote "The City on the Edge of Forever," a standout TOS episode that recently was released in comic book form based on the writer's original draft.

Isaac Asimov A friend of Roddenberry's, the famed writer never contributed a script to the franchise, but he was hired as "Special Science Consultant" for *Star Trek: The Motion Picture*.

Larry Niven Sci-fi novelist Larry Niven adapted one of his short stories featuring the feline Kzinti for *The Animated Series*.

Theodore Sturgeon The acclaimed science-fiction and horror writer penned the TOS episodes "Shore Leave" and "Amok Time."

George Clayton Johnson The novelist who created the film and TV franchise *Logan's Run* also wrote the TOS episode "The Man Trap."

Robert Bloch Hugo Award-winning Bloch was best known for his novel, *Psycho*, which Alfred Hitchcock made into the film classic. Bloch wrote three episodes for The Original Series: "What Are Little Girls Made of?" "Catspaw," and "Wolf in the Fold."

PLAY WITHIN A PLAY

"THE PLAY'S THE THING WHEREIN I'LL CATCH THE CONSCIENCE OF THE KING," SAID HAMLET, WHEN HE WAS TRYING TO SEE THE MURDEROUS GUILT IN HIS UNCLE'S REACTION TO A PLAY. *STAR TREK* USED THIS DEVICE OF TELLING A STORY WITHIN A STORY TO REFLECT THE LARGER THEME IN SEVERAL EPISODES, MOST NOTABLY IN AN EPISODE THAT TOOK ITS INSPIRATION FROM *HAMLET*'S FAMOUS LINE.

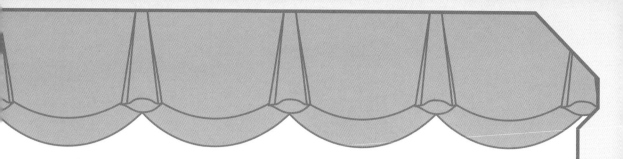

"The Inner Light" Picard lived an entire lifetime while rendered unconscious by an alien probe.

TNG

"The Menagerie" The Talosians beamed mental illusions to the *Enterprise* that told the story of Captain Pike's first visit to their planet, in order to justify Spock bringing Pike back.

TOS

"Frame of Mind" While Riker starred in a play written by Dr. Crusher, he was abducted by aliens in an experience that forced him to live out the play's events.

TNG

"The Royale" Aliens created what they thought would be a paradise for the last member of a twenty-first-century Earth ship from the pages of a book, but it became his prison. The *Enterprise*-D crew became stuck in the simulation, but the ending of the book gave them a clue of how to escape the same fate.

TNG

"Elementary, Dear Data"/"Ship in a Bottle" Data unknowingly created a sentient hologram of Professor Moriarty in an attempt to have an equal antagonist for his own Sherlock Holmes. Years later, Moriarty believed himself to have escaped the holodeck, but was in fact in a holosimulation of the universe outside the *Enterprise*-D.

TNG

"The Conscience of the King" The Karidian Company of Players enacted *Hamlet* and *Macbeth* as Kirk searched for a mass murderer.

TOS

"The Storyteller" O'Brien found himself the unwilling spiritual leader in a village living in fear of a fictional creation intended to unite the people. Bashir helped O'Brien rewrite the heroic falsehood the villagers believed to allow a better suited leader to step forward.

DS9

"Far Beyond the Stars" Sisko experienced visions of himself and his crew as 1950s science-fiction writers, as he struggled with his doubts about his role in the Dominion war.

DS9

"The Killing Game" When taken prisoner by the Hirogen, the *Voyager* crew was unwittingly forced into battle simulations set at various points in Federation history. Once they regained their stolen memories, they had to play the part of a real resistance to take back the ship.

VGR

"These Are the Voyages . . ." While experiencing a moral crisis, Commander Riker watched the events that led to the founding of the Federation on the holodeck through the eyes of the crew of *Enterprise* NX-01.

ENT

LIST #60 / COURTS-MARTIAL

IN THE MILITARY, A COURT-MARTIAL IS THE MILITARY COURT TO DETERMINE THE INNOCENCE OR GUILT OF A CREW MEMBER OR OFFICER. WHILE MOST MEMBERS OF STARFLEET ARE ABOVE REPROACH, EVEN DECORATED OFFICERS LIKE CAPTAIN KIRK HAVE FOUND THEMSELVES HAVING TO JUSTIFY THEIR ACTIONS . . . BUT NOT ALWAYS IN A FORMAL FEDERATION PROCEDURE.

"Court Martial" Accused of negligence in the death of his former friend Ben Finney, Kirk had to prove his innocence by determining that Finney was still alive.

TOS

"Turnabout Intruder" Using ancient technology, an embittered former lover transferred her mind into Kirk's body and then tried to have Spock and Kirk (in her body) charged with mutiny.

TOS

"The Magicks of Megas-Tu" The Salem witch trials were reversed when a planet of magicians placed the *Enterprise* crew on trial for humanity's persecution of their sorcerous race.

TAS

"The Drumhead" After an explosion and suspected Romulan involvement, Admiral Norah Satie conducted a witch hunt aboard the *Enterprise*-D.

TNG

"The Measure of a Man" Data resigned his commission rather than be subjected to invasive testing, forcing Picard to convene a formal hearing to prove the android was a sentient being and not the property of Starfleet.

TNG

"The First Duty" A tragic accident at Starfleet Academy saw the exemplary cadets of Nova Squadron under investigation for actions that led to the death of a friend and fellow cadet.

TNG

"Hard Time" O'Brien was falsely accused of spying on the Argrathi people and sentenced to twenty years of hard time in the form of implanted memories.

DS9

"Encounter at Farpoint" Q's first meeting with Captain Picard and the crew of the *Enterprise*-D saw him placing them on trial as a proxy for humanity and all its past savagery.

TNG

"The Menagerie" Spock requested a formal hearing to explain his actions after he commandeered the *U.S.S. Enterprise* to take his former commanding officer, Captain Christopher Pike, to the forbidden planet Talos IV.

TOS

"Blaze of Glory" Michael Eddington was a Maquis sympathizer who defected while stealing industrial replicators slated for delivery to the Cardassians. Sisko captured the former Starfleet officer and Eddington was court-martialed.

DS9

"Tribunal" O'Brien was arrested by Cardassians for aiding the Maquis and was placed on trial in a Cardassian system of justice that assumed defendants were guilty until proven innocent.

DS9

"Rules of Engagement" The Klingon Empire attempted to extradite Worf, claiming he had destroyed a transport ship of innocent Klingon citizens.

DS9

"Death Wish" When the Q known as Quinn wanted to die, Janeway convened a hearing aboard *Voyager* to mediate. Q called witnesses that included Commander Riker and Sir Isaac Newton, but ultimately Janeway ruled Quinn had the right to leave the Continuum and die.

VGR

Star Trek IV: The Voyage Home Admiral Kirk and the *Enterprise* senior staff were brought up on numerous charges after commandeering the ship to save Spock. All charges but one were dropped in light of their actions saving Earth from a cataclysmic event, but the admiral was demoted to captain and reassigned to the new *Enterprise*-A.

Star Trek VI: The Undiscovered Country Captain Kirk and Dr. McCoy were brought before a Klingon tribunal and accused of being party to the murder of Chancellor Gorkon.

IDENTITY CRISIS

IN FOLKLORE, SEEING YOUR DOPPELGÄNGER—EXACT DUPLICATE—IS CONSIDERED BAD LUCK. WHILE NOT ALWAYS THE CASE IN *STAR TREK*, MANY TIMES, FINDING A PERSON WHO IS ONE'S MIRROR IMAGE COULD BE DISCONCERTING AT THE LEAST, POTENTIALLY FATAL AT WORST, AND ULTIMATELY A COMMON OCCURRENCE ACROSS THE FRANCHISE.

James T. Kirk The captain was split into good and evil selves in "The Enemy Within," saw a robot duplicate created in "What Are Little Girls Made Of?" and exchanged bodies with his former lover, Janice Lester in "Turnabout Intruder."

TOS

William Riker A transporter accident duplicated Will Riker and left the new version of the officer stranded on a planet for eight years. The resulting Riker took their middle name, Tom, to distinguish himself from his "brother."

TNG "SECOND CHANCES"

Spock The science officer was cloned to a gigantic size by a clone of Dr. Stavos Keniclius, a scientist from Earth during the Eugenics Wars.

TAS "THE INFINITE VULCAN"

Data The *Enterprise*-D second officer's creator made two other androids that shared Data's image: the evil Lore and the less-advanced B-4.

TNG "DATALORE"/*STAR TREK NEMESIS*

Jean-Luc Picard A Romulan plot cloned a younger version of Picard, who became the leader of the Remans and then took over the Romulan government before dying in his battle with Picard.

STAR TREK NEMESIS

Miles O'Brien The Paradans created a replicant of Chief O'Brien with the intention of assassinating someone during peace talks at Deep Space 9.

DS9 "WHISPERS"

Tasha Yar When Tasha Yar from an alternate timeline went back in time to help the *Enterprise*-C fight the battle of Narendra III, she survived but was captured by Romulans. To save the others, she became a Romulan's consort and bore him a daughter, Sela, who ultimately betrayed her. Sela's uncanny resemblance to her mother stunned the *Enterprise*-D crew when she first encountered them.

TNG "YESTERDAY'S *ENTERPRISE*"/"REDEMPTION"

Kahless The clerics at the Klingons' sacred Temple of Boreth cloned the legendary Klingon figure from a blade with his blood. Their goal was to have him lead the Klingon people again.

DS9 "THE SWORD OF KAHLESS"

U.S.S. Voyager crew The entire crew of *Voyager* and the ship itself was duplicated by the unique mimetic substance known as "silver blood."

VGR "DEMON"/"COURSE: OBLIVION"

MIRROR UNIVERSE

OVER THE COURSE OF THREE SERIES, NUMEROUS *STAR TREK* CHARACTERS WERE DUPLICATED IN EPISODES SET IN THE MIRROR UNIVERSE.

TOS

James T. Kirk
Spock
Leonard McCoy
Uhura
Scotty
Sulu
Chekov
Marlena Moreau

ENT

Jonathan Archer
T'Pol
Charles Tucker
Travis Mayweather
Malcolm Reed
Phlox
Hoshi Sato
Porthos
Zefram Cochrane
Maximilian Forrest

DS9

Benjamin Sisko

Jennifer Sisko

Miles ("Smiley") O'Brien

Kira Nerys (Intendant)

Odo

Worf

Julian Bashir

Jadzia Dax

Ezri Dax

Quark

Rom

Nog

Bareil Antos

Leeta

Garak

Vic Fontaine

VGR

Tuvok

LIST #63 — SHIPS IN A BOTTLE

IN TELEVISION PARLANCE, A "BOTTLE" SHOW IS ONE IN WHICH THE ACTION IS ENTIRELY CONTAINED TO EXISTING SETS. THIS IS USUALLY DONE AS A COST-SAVING MEASURE TO KEEP THE PRODUCTION FROM HAVING TO BUILD NEW SETS OR SCOUT EXPENSIVE LOCATIONS. SOME OF THESE EPISODES FOCUS ON CHARACTER DEVELOPMENT OR DRAMA, RESULTING IN THE STRONGEST STORIES IN THE SERIES. OTHER TIMES . . . THEY ARE LESS SUCCESSFUL. BUT GENERALLY SPEAKING, THEY ARE OFTEN MEMORABLE.

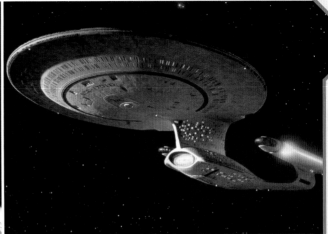

TOS

"The Naked Time"

"The Doomsday Machine"

"The Mark of Gideon"

TNG

"Shades of Gray"

"The Offspring"

"Clues"

"Conundrum"

DS9

"Duet"

"The Wire"

"Facets"

VGR

"Jetrel"

"Twisted"

ENT

"A Night in Sickbay"

"Catwalk"

"Daedalus"

UNDERCOVER AGENTS

"The name is Kirk. James Kirk."

THOUGH THE BELOVED CAPTAIN NEVER ASKED FOR A MARTINI SHAKEN, NOT STIRRED, HE AND OTHER STARFLEET OFFICERS ENCOUNTERED THEIR FAIR SHARE OF GALACTIC INTRIGUE. FROM HOLODECK ADVENTURES TO ALIEN INTELLIGENCE-GATHERING AGENCIES, SOME OF THE MOST SECRET AGENTS IN THE GALAXY INCLUDE:

Kirk Captain Kirk seemed to be acting irrationally when he ordered the *Enterprise* to cross into the Romulan Neutral Zone, but there was a method to his madness; he was acting on orders from the Federation to acquire a Romulan cloaking device.

TOS "THE *ENTERPRISE* INCIDENT"

Seska A Cardassian spy surgically altered to look Bajoran, Seska infiltrated Chakotay's Maquis crew and began a relationship with him. She then collaborated with the Kazon when they were stranded in the Delta Quadrant.

VGR "BASICS"

Talok A Romulan spy who worked secretly with V'Las, head of the Vulcan High Command, to begin a reunification of their two peoples. But in truth, Talok was attempting to help the Romulans conquer Vulcan.

ENT "KIR'SHARA"

Thelev This Orion agent posed as a member of the Andorian ambassadorial delegation to Babel where he killed the Tellarite ambassador Gav and gravely wounded Kirk before being apprehended.

TOS "JOURNEY TO BABEL"

Tal Shiar The Romulan elite intelligence agency was greatly feared by its own people. Though they technically reported to the Romulan praetor, they took on covert missions under their own authority, circumventing the Senate. Counselor Deanna Troi once pretended to be a Tal Shiar agent aboard a Romulan ship to help a defector escape to the Federation.

TNG "FACE OF THE ENEMY"

Picard Captain Jean-Luc Picard took on the alias of the smuggler Galen in order to uncover the plot of Vulcan isolationists looting archaeological digs for the famed Stone of Gol.

TNG "GAMBIT"

T'Pel Renowned Vulcan ambassador T'Pel was in actuality Subcommander Selok. After years of infiltrating the Federation, she faked her death in a transporter accident to be extracted by a Romulan vessel.

TNG "DATA'S DAY"

Arne Darvin The Klingon agent was surgically altered to look Human and posed as an assistant to the Federation undersecretary for agriculture. When Kirk and the *Enterprise* crew exposed him, Darvin was forced from the Klingon Empire in disgrace. He eventually landed on Cardassia and used the Bajoran Orb of Time to go back into the past to kill Kirk.

TOS "THE TROUBLE WITH TRIBBLES"/
DS9 "TRIALS AND TRIBBLE-ATIONS"

Elim Garak/Enabran Tain On Deep Space 9, Garak attempted to hide behind the facade of being a simple tailor. In fact, he had once been the protégé of his father, Enabran Tain, head of the Cardassian secret intelligence agency known as the **Obsidian Order**. Garak was known for his interrogation skills and his ability to lie convincingly. Tain headed the Obsidian Order for twenty years; the only Cardassian to live so long in the position.

DS9 "THE WIRE"/
"IN PURGATORY'S SHADOW"

Section 31 Officially, Section 31 doesn't exist. Only a few even know the black-ops agency's name. It was formed in the earliest days of Earth's Starfleet and recruited Malcolm Reed before he served aboard *Enterprise* NX-01. Centuries later, Luther Sloan tried to recruit Dr. Julian Bashir of Deep Space 9. The doctor initially refused, but Captain Sisko suggested he might be able to spy on the spies by joining. Section 31 was found to be responsible for the morphogenic virus infecting Odo and the Founders in an effort to cripple the Dominion's leaders, though Bashir found a cure. Section 31 was exposed by Khan Noonien Singh in the *Kelvin* Timeline.

ENT "AFFLICTION"/DS9 "INQUISITION"/"EXTREME MEASURES"

MIND GAMES

IT'S A BIG UNIVERSE . . . AND WHILE HUMANS ARE FAIRLY HIGH ON THE EVOLUTIONARY LADDER, THERE ARE SOME SPECIES WHOSE MENTAL DEVELOPMENT IS SO GREAT THAT THEY CAN CONTROL OTHER MINDS OR RESIST MENTAL CONTROL THEMSELVES. SOME DEVICES AND EVEN CREATURES CAN UTILIZE FORMS OF MIND CONTROL. WHEN TRAVELING THE GALAXY, IT'S GOOD TO KEEP AN OPEN MIND, BUT MAKE SURE YOU CAN STILL CLOSE IT TOO.

Neural neutralizer The device used on the Tantalus V penal colony for rehabilitation proved all too easy to adapt for more sinister purposes. After a mind-meld with Spock, Dr. Simon Van Gelder dismantled the device.

TOS "DAGGER OF THE MIND"

Denevan neural parasites Jellyfish-like flying creatures, these parasites create intense pain and insanity in their victims, even when their commands are obeyed.

TOS "OPERATION: ANNHILATE!"

Omicron Ceti spores These spores from the pod plants don't technically control minds but infection by the spores creates perfect health and euphoria in people as long as they never left the planet.

TOS "THIS SIDE OF PARADISE"

Talosians The realistic illusions projected by the Talosians are so feared that travel to their planet was banned. Their reach is vast, and they can destroy a ship by mentally showing a victim the wrong button or lever to push.

TOS "THE MENAGERIE"

Transmuter Sylvia and Korob's transmuter allowed them to reshape reality to their mental image as well as exert mental control over another person.

TOS "CATSPAW"

Ktarian game The game, brought to the *Enterprise*-D by Commander Riker, has an addictive component that stimulates the brain's pleasure centers, making the user want to do nothing but play.

TNG "THE GAME"

Ceti Alpha eels Native to Ceti Alpha V, these worms burrow into the cerebral cortex and make their victims susceptible to suggestion.

STAR TREK II: THE WRATH OF KHAN

Landru The computer that once managed the planet Beta III was given the brain patterns of its creator, and it had the ability to "absorb" an individual's will.

TOS "RETURN OF THE ARCHONS"

Redjac The noncorporeal being could possess both people and objects. It fed on pain and fear and caused its hosts to murder to produce those emotions.

TOS "WOLF IN THE FOLD"

Elasian tears The biochemical compound in the tears of Elasian women causes any man who touches the tears to be romantically enslaved with the woman.

TOS "ELAAN OF TROYIUS"

Twenty-fourth-century neural parasites Several high-ranking Starfleet Command personnel were found to be under the control of intelligent neural parasites.

TNG "CONSPIRACY"

E-band emissions Geordi La Forge's VISOR was compromised when he was kidnapped by Romulans and E-band emissions allowed them to trigger mental suggestions.

TNG "THE MIND'S EYE"

Kironide This rare extract gives psychokinetic powers to humanoids, allowing the user to command another to do their bidding. The controlled individual will seem aware of the control, but cannot fight it.

TOS "PLATO'S STEPCHILDREN"

Neural implant Tieran, a warlord who possessed host after host through a neural implant, possessed Kes on *Voyager* until a mind-meld with Tuvok allowed her to break free.

VGR "WARLORD"

If one is good, two will be better . . . at least as far as Hollywood is concerned. There were so many great concepts and ideas in The Original Series and then The Next Generation, it was no wonder the writers of later episodes and films drew inspiration from previous series to revisit storylines that resonated with fans.

TOS "Space Seed"/*Star Trek II: The Wrath of Khan*/*Star Trek Into Darkness* Once Khan Noonien Singh was exiled on Ceti Alpha VI, it left things open for him to return. The second feature film brought him back in a big way and made him perhaps the ultimate *Star Trek* antagonist, notable enough to serve as an inspiration for the *Kelvin* Timeline as well.

***Star Trek: First Contact*/ENT "Regeneration"** Despite being set a century before the time of *The Next Generation*, the Borg made an appearance in *Enterprise*. Stemming from the events of *Star Trek: First Contact*, Borg drones were discovered, and Archer's crew was forced to stop them.

TOS "Mirror, Mirror"/DS9 "Crossover"/ "Through the Looking Glass"/"Shattered Mirror"/"Resurrection"/"The Emperor's New Cloak"/ENT "In a Mirror, Darkly" Both *Deep Space Nine* and *Enterprise* utilized the Mirror Universe established in The Original Series by showing the evil alternate versions of DS9, *Enterprise* NX-01, and even *Voyager* crew members. *Enterprise* tied their mirror episode in with another episode of The Original Series, "The Tholian Web," making it double the sequel.

TOS "The City on the Edge of Forever"/ TAS "Yesteryear" Utilizing only the time-travel device from "The City on the Edge of Forever," the Guardian of Forever, this animated sequel tugged on the heartstrings much as the live-action episode had done. This time Spock had to let someone die to correct the timeline, and it was his beloved pet. While *The Animated Series* is not considered canon, this episode was subtly referenced in future episodes of the franchise allowing many elements a backdoor entrance to canon.

TOS "Shore Leave"/TAS "Once Upon a Planet" When the Caretaker of the "Shore Leave" planet died, the computer, tired of serving guests, wanted to hijack the *Enterprise* to find computers similar to itself.

TOS "The Trouble with Tribbles/TAS "More Tribbles, More Troubles"/DS9 "Trials and Tribble-ations" You can't keep a good tribble down, no matter how much trouble it causes! These adorably overwhelming balls of fluff showed up in *The Animated Series*, cameoed in *Star Trek III: The Search for Spock* and then the Deep Space 9 crew went back in time to Kirk's encounter with the tribbles. Tribbles were also around in the *Kelvin* Timeline, where one showed up on Scotty's desk and another served as a subject for Dr. McCoy, who used it to test the properties of Khan's blood.

TOS "The Naked Time"/TNG "The Naked Now" During the initial year of *Star Trek: The Next Generation*, several episode themes were callbacks to ones from The Original Series. "The Naked Now" was a direct sequel in the threat that was a descendent of the previous polywater intoxication and the manner in which it revealed the crew expressing hidden or inner desires.

TOS "Errand of Mercy"/"The Trouble with Tribbles"/"Day of the Dove"/DS9 "Blood Oath" Kang, Koloth and Kor were all Klingons who had encountered Kirk during The Original Series. At some unknown point, they also had encountered Curzon Dax. Years later, they joined with the new Dax symbiont host, Jadzia, to fulfill a blood oath to kill a mutual enemy.

TOS "Space Seed"/TNG "Datalore"/ENT "The Augments" Weaving together threads from The Original Series and *The Next Generation*, *Enterprise* presented a tale of the Eugenics Wars and the ancestor of Data's creator, Dr. Arik Soong.

***Star Trek VI: The Undiscovered Country*/VGR "Flashback"** *The Undiscovered Country* saw Captain Sulu commanding the *U.S.S. Excelsior* onscreen for the first time. Years later, Captain Kathryn Janeway and Tuvok would flash back via a mind-meld to Tuvok's memories, and relive some of Tuvok's service under Captain Sulu.

BEAM US UP, SCOTTY!

"I signed on this ship to practice medicine, not to have my atoms scattered back and forth across space by this gadget."

–Dr. Leonard "Bones" McCoy

DESPITE DR. MCCOY'S MISGIVINGS, TRANSPORTERS WERE, AS GEORDI SAID ON TNG, THE SAFEST WAY TO TRAVEL. STILL, SOMETIMES THINGS DID GO WRONG, LEADING TO SURPRISING RESULTS THAT PROVED DR. MCCOY MAY HAVE BEEN RIGHT TO AVOID TRANSPORTER TRAVEL.

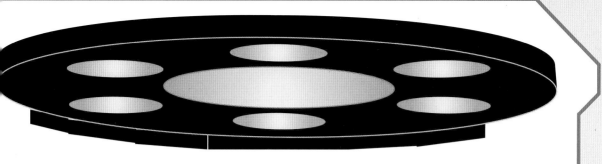

"The Enemy Within" Captain Kirk was split into two Kirks: one good, yet passive and indecisive; and one savage. TOS

"Mirror, Mirror" A freak ion storm while mid-transport sent four of the *Enterprise* crew to an evil Mirror Universe. TOS

"Tuvix" Enzymes of an alien orchid caused two unlikely crewmates—Tuvok and Neelix—to fuse into a new being named Tuvix. To get her crew members back, Janeway was forced to end Tuvix's existence. VGR

"Rascals" Picard, Ro, Guinan, and Keiko physically de-aged to young children, while their minds remained adult. TNG

Star Trek: The Motion Picture The newly refit *Enterprise* was unable to capture Commander Sonak and another officer's patterns. The two rematerialized into one form that died quickly.

"The Next Phase" Geordi and Ro were believed dead after a transporter malfunction. They were actually cloaked by chronitons and managed to reappear in the middle of their own memorial service. TNG

"Our Man Bashir" When most of the DS9 command crew was beamed out of an exploding runabout, the computer had to store their patterns to save them. It did so in the middle of Bashir's 1960s holosuite program. DS9

"Second Chances" William Riker was accidentally duplicated when a distortion field bounced a second transporter beam back to the surface of Nervala IV. TNG

"Drone" A transporter accident created a twenty-ninth-century Borg drone from the Doctor's mobile emitter and Seven of Nine's nanoprobes. VGR

"Daedalus" The inventor of the transporter used *Enterprise* NX-01 in a dangerous attempt to bring back his son who was lost during a transporter test. ENT

"Realm of Fear" Barclay claimed to see creatures in the transporter beam, which turned out to be crewmen lost from another ship. TNG

"Relics" Scotty managed to keep his pattern in a diagnostic loop for over seventy-five years until he could be rescued from the crashed *Jenolen*. TNG

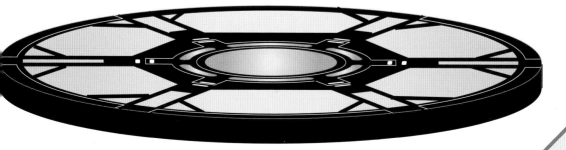

THE RESET BUTTON

Modern television shows are far more serialized than when The Original Series or even Voyager was on the air. At that time, episodic television usually tried to keep the status quo. Having a main cast member die or changing the format of a show involved new casting, additional sets, and story changes. But science fiction has the benefit of using technology, time travel, or even mind control to reset the status quo by the end of an episode, making sure that a character could die, but still be in next week's show.

"Tomorrow Is Yesterday" The *Enterprise* took a pilot back in time to ensure his son would lead a crucial space mission in the future.

TOS

"Cause and Effect" The *Enterprise*-D was caught in a time distortion that kept destroying the ship until the crew could break the loop and journey on completely unaware of the situation.

TNG

"Future Imperfect" Riker's future as a captain with a family turned out to be an alien child's holographic technology.

TNG

"Parallels" Worf encountered numerous parallel universes, many with dire outcomes for the Federation, before being returned to his proper reality.

TNG

"All Good Things . . . " Q sent Picard through three points in time to save Earth from an anti-time cataclysm.

TNG

"Storm Front" Archer and the *Enterprise* NX-01 crew saved Earth from a timeline where the Nazis won World War II.

ENT

"Year of Hell" *Voyager* endured a punishing year of death and damage until Captain Janeway destroyed a Krenim time weapon that restored things to their proper reality.

VGR

"Timeless" An older Chakotay and Kim traveled back in time to prevent a mistake that would result in *Voyager*'s untimely destruction.

VGR

"Endgame" Like Chakotay and Kim before her, Admiral Janeway journeyed from the future to change the past and bring her crew home earlier than their original timeline.

VGR

"Vanishing Point" Ensign Hoshi Sato hallucinated her own death and the sabotage of *Enterprise* NX-01 while trapped in a transporter pattern buffer for 8.3 seconds.

ENT

Star Trek: First Contact The Borg went back in time to alter history, resulting in Earth's assimilation. The *Enterprise*-E followed the Borg back in time to stop them.

STORIES NEVER TOLD

FOR AS MANY STORIES AS *STAR TREK* EPISODES HAVE SHARED, THERE ARE AS MANY MORE THAT REMAIN UNTOLD . . . AT LEAST FOR THE MOMENT.

Eugenics Wars The wars fought between Humans and the genetically superior Augments were never shown on screen, though Kirk and Archer both met survivors of Earth's "supermen."

TOS "SPACE SEED"/ENT "THE AUGMENTS"

World War III/Colonel Green Kirk and Spock met a replica of the infamous colonel who killed millions with radiation poisoning on Excalbia, but viewers never saw the horrors Humans unleashed on themselves and the planet.

TOS "THE SAVAGE CURTAIN"

Battle of Cheron The battle that ended the Romulan War in 2160 was fought by an alliance of the founding members of the Federation (Humans, Vulcans, Tellarites, and Andorians) against the Romulan Star Empire.

TNG "THE DEFECTOR"/ENT "IN A MIRROR, DARKLY"

Tomed Incident An unknown but devastating encounter with the Romulan Star Empire led to the Treaty of Algernon, which banned Starfleet from developing cloaking technology.

TNG "THE NEUTRAL ZONE"

Khitomer massacre Romulans, with the aid of a Klingon traitor, killed over four thousand members of this Klingon colony, including Worf's father.

TNG "SINS OF THE FATHER"

Lieutenant Kirk of the *U.S.S. Farragut* While Kirk encountered the dikironium cloud creature again when he became a captain, it was never seen how he "performed with uncommon bravery" the first time he met it as a lieutenant.

TOS "OBSESSIONS"

Spock's service under Pike Spock served for eleven years under Captain Christopher Pike, including the alluded-to incident at Rigel VII, but his career is a mystery.

TOS "THE MENAGERIE"

Emony Dax meets Dr. McCoy The Emony host of the Dax symbiont encountered Leonard McCoy at the University of Mississippi in a memorable, though mysterious, encounter.

DS9 "TRIALS AND TRIBBLE-ATIONS"

Jean-Luc Picard meets Guinan The past between these two members of the *Enterprise*-D crew remains one of the greatest mysteries in the *Star Trek* universe.

Battle of Axanar The tactics used by Garth of Izar became required reading at the academy after this Federation battle.

TOS "WHOM GODS DESTROY"

Setlik III massacre Cardassian troops killed over a hundred civilians, drawing the *U.S.S. Rutledge* into a firefight and rescue mission.

TNG "THE WOUNDED"

Narendra III The crew of the *Enterprise*-C went back in time to face certain death, though at least one person survived.

TNG "YESTERDAY'S *ENTERPRISE*"

Star Trek: Phase II In 1977, *Star Trek* as a film was not yet a reality. Gene Roddenberry pitched Phase II, which introduced new characters and concepts. Phase II never happened, but much of it was developed into *Star Trek: The Motion Picture* and later *Star Trek: The Next Generation*.

FUTURE LEADERS

Cadets enrolled in Starfleet Academy undergo rigorous mental and physical training. The program generally lasts four years, though some cadets enroll in longer curriculums. While the different *Star Trek* series have focused on the adventures of academy alumni, occasionally active cadets have made an appearance or had an entire episode centered around the formative years of these future Starfleet officers.

"Shore Leave" Kirk met a replica of his old academy nemesis, Finnegan, and got to exact some satisfying revenge for numerous pranks.

TOS

"Coming of Age" Wesley Crusher took his Starfleet Academy entrance exam and failed. He was disappointed in himself until Picard revealed that he too had failed on the first try.

TNG

"Q2" Once Icheb was freed from the Borg collective, he worked to gain entrance to Starfleet Academy, passing his history exam just before Q Junior appeared on the ship.

VGR

"The First Duty" Wesley's cadet team, Nova Squadron, was involved in a fatal accident, forcing the cadet to choose between loyalty to his friends and the truth.

TNG

"Heart of Stone" Nog despaired of a possible future life like his father's, and pushed for Sisko's recommendation to be the first Ferengi in Starfleet Academy.

DS9

Star Trek II: The Wrath of Khan Admiral Kirk and a ship full of cadets had to take the *U.S.S. Enterprise* out to face Kirk's archenemy Khan.

"Homefront/Paradise Lost" Acadamy Cadet Nog introduced Sisko to the members of Red Squad, a group of elite academy cadets who unwittingly helped the Changelings launch a coup on Earth.

DS9

"Valiant" Red Squad was assigned a training mission aboard the *U.S.S. Valiant* and were trapped behind enemy lines, where they rescued Nog and Jake. Nog, in his eagerness to join the elite crew, almost led himself and his friend into the crew's grim fate.

DS9

"Final Mission" Weeks before Wesley Crusher left to attend the academy, he and Picard were involved in a crash on an inhospitable moon. Crusher saved Picard's life, earning the captain's acknowledgment that the cadet would be missed.

TNG

"In the Flesh" The *Voyager* crew encountered a replica of Starfleet Academy created by Species 8472 as a training ground, including a replica Boothby, the gardener who was a mentor to both Captains Picard and Janeway.

VGR

***Star Trek* (2009) The *Kelvin* Timeline** James Kirk had to be goaded into entering Starfleet Academy on a dare. Once there, he repeated history from a different timeline by beating the *Kobayashi Maru* training scenario and meeting the fellow cadets that would ultimately become his senior staff on the *Enterprise*.

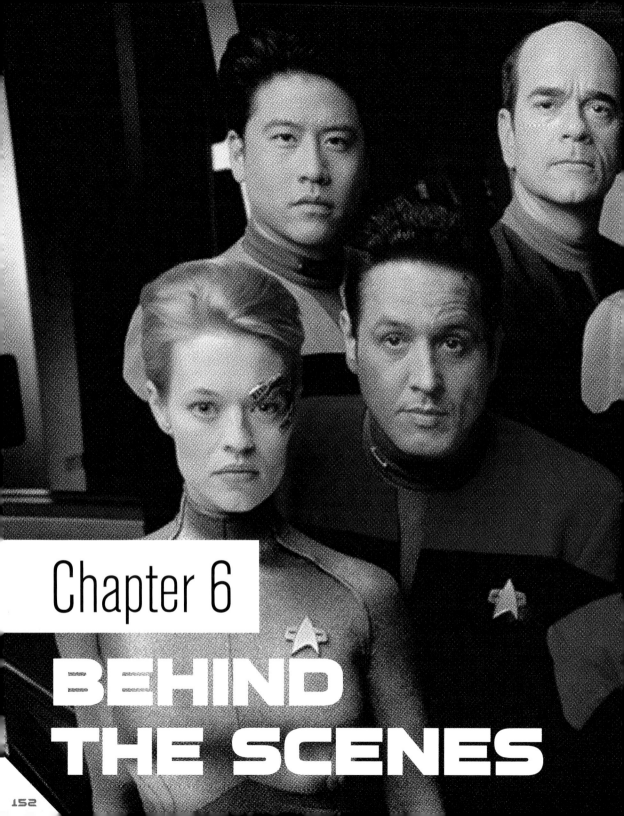

Chapter 6
BEHIND
THE SCENES

FIGHT ON VASQUEZ ROCKS

Almost as iconic as the *Starship Enterprise* herself, the jutting cliffs of the Vasquez Rocks Natural Area Park an hour north of Los Angeles are instantly familiar to *Star Trek* fans. Once the hideout of California bandit Tiburcio Vasquez, the rocks have played host to filming "centuries" of *Star Trek* shows and homages to *Star Trek* in pop culture, including:

The so-called "amusement park planet"
TOS "SHORE LEAVE"

Landing site of Lazarus's ship
TOS "THE ALTERNATIVE FACTOR"

Kirk fights the Gorn captain
TOS "ARENA"

Capella IV
TOS "FRIDAY'S CHILD"

Vulcan landscape
STAR TREK (2009)

Mintaka III
TNG "WHO WATCHES THE WATCHERS"

Tarok, moon that the Kazon-Olga used as a training ground
VGR "INITIATIONS"

Vulcan peak
STAR TREK IV: THE VOYAGE HOME

Holographic simulation of Xyrillian home world
ENT "UNEXPECTED"

IN STAGES

Since the beginning of The Original Series, the sound stages at Paramount Pictures in Hollywood, California, have been the main home of *Star Trek*. The Original Series was filmed at Desilu Studios (Lucille Ball and Desi Arnaz's company), which became part of Paramount in 1967. Every television series, including *Star Trek: Discovery*, has filmed at the famed Hollywood studio.

Stage 31 Originally Desilu Stage 9, this single stage housed the bulk of the *U.S.S. Enterprise* interiors, including the bridge, transporter room, sickbay, and engineering.

Stage 32 Originally Desilu Stage 10, this swing set was used for planet landscapes. During filming of *Star Trek Nemesis*, the Romulan Senate and wedding pavilion scenes were filmed here.

Stage 5 First used as Gary Seven's apartment in "Assignment Earth," this stage also housed some of the interiors of the cloud city Stratos, the Sarpedion library and ice cavern, and Flint's castle in The Original Series. For *Star Trek: The Wrath of Khan*, it held the Regula I lab and cavern sets. It also housed interiors for the *U.S.S. Excelsior* and Klingon ships in *The Undiscovered Country* as well as the *Enterprise*-E in *Insurrection*.

Stage 8 Season one of *The Next Generation* found the bridge and captain's ready room on Stage 6. The second season moved these sets and added Ten Forward to the larger Stage 8, where they remained for the duration of TNG filming. After *Star Trek Generations*, the old set was struck and the bridge for *Voyager*, along with its ready room and briefing room, were built here. When *Voyager* ended, the stages became the home for *Enterprise*'s sickbay, mess hall, crew quarters and captain's dining room. After the end of *Enterprise*, years passed with no *Star Trek* production utilizing the stage, until the 2009 *Star Trek* film used it once again.

Stage 9 The engineering room from *Star Trek: The Motion Picture* and the *Enterprise*-A bridge and other rooms from *Star Trek IV: The Voyage Home* through *Star Trek VI: The Undiscovered Country* were housed in Stage 9. It then became corridors, sickbay, the transporter room, and living quarters on *The Next Generation* before housing engineering and sickbay for *Voyager*, and ultimately becoming a swing set and cave and planet set for *Star Trek: Enterprise*.

Stages 14/15 Combining to become one of the largest soundstages in Hollywood, these two stages were the settings for the Genesis Planet in *The Search for Spock* and the deflector dish Borg battle in *First Contact*.

Stage 17 First used in *Star Trek: The Motion Picture*, Stage 17 became the enormous three-story set for *Deep Space Nine*'s Promenade.

Stage 18 Famous films such as *Sunset Blvd.* and Hitchcock's *Rear Window* were filmed on Stage 18. *Star Trek* fans saw it more as "Planet Hell," the rocky cave set for *Deep Space Nine*.

B-Tank When not used for filming, this parking lot at Paramount Pictures sits right beside the Gene Roddenberry building. But it's better known to *Star Trek* fans as the spot where a Klingon bird-of-prey crash-landed in the San Francisco Bay in *The Voyage Home* and where Data took an underwater walk in *Insurrection.*

Paramount Director's Building Often, other locations on the Paramount lot could be used for exteriors. The Director's Building—now known as the Schulberg Building—doubled as the Ekosian headquarters in the TOS episode "Patterns of Force."

Marlene Dietrich Building The NASA building in "Assignment: Earth" was actually behind the Dietrich Building.

Paramount Theater The lobby of the studio's movie theater served as the location of the meeting of the newly forming Coalition of Planets in the *Enterprise* episode "Terra Prime."

PLANET HELL

Stage 16 on the Paramount Pictures lot has been the home of many sets for films and television series, from *Bonanza* to Alfred Hitchcock's *Vertigo*. But beginning with *Star Trek: The Next Generation* and through *Star Trek: Discovery*, Stage 16 became almost every alien or cavernous landscape imaginable. Nicknamed "Planet Hell," the soundstage became the *Star Trek* productions' swing set, a Hollywood term for a set that was redressed or reconfigured frequently as opposed to a fixed set like the starship's bridge.

Eventually, *Star Trek: Voyager* staff paid homage to this in-joke by having the *Voyager* crew nickname the harsh breeding planet of the reptohumanioids "Planet Hell" in the episode "Parturition." This, of course, was filmed on Stage 16. These other notable locations were among the many caves, tunnels, alien cities and planetary landscapes Planet Hell hosted:

Q's courtroom TNG "Encounter at Farpoint"

Rura Penthe *Star Trek VI: The Undiscovered Country*

Galorndon Core TNG "The Enemy"

Vagra II TNG "Skin of Evil"

Holodeck Cliffs TNG "Bloodlines"

Turkana IV TNG "Legacy"

Mintaka III TNG "Who Watches the Watchers"

Mab-Bu VI moon TNG "Power Play"

U.S.S. Potemkin crash TNG "Second Chances"

Romulus caves TNG "Unification"

Bajoran Fire Caves DS9 "What You Leave Behind"

Ba'ku caves *STAR TREK: Insurrection*

Paxau Resort Holoprogram VGR

NEW YORK, NEW WORLD

THE PARAMOUNT BACKLOT CONTAINED A LARGE OUTDOOR SET THAT MIMICKED SEVERAL METROPOLITAN AREAS AND WAS DUBBED "NEW YORK STREET." ALTHOUGH THE ORIGINAL VERSION OF THE BACKLOT BURNED DOWN IN 1983 WHILE SCENES FROM *THE SEARCH FOR SPOCK* WERE FILMING IN THE SOUNDSTAGE BESIDE IT, A NEW STREET DEBUTED WHILE *THE NEXT GENERATION* WAS FILMING ON THE LOT. TELEVISION SHOWS, FILMS, AND EVEN COMMERCIALS HAVE USED IT FOR ANY NUMBER OF URBAN CITIES AND TIME PERIODS. *STAR TREK* OFTEN DID AS WELL.

1893 San Francisco
TNG "Time's Arrow"

1941 San Francisco (holographic)
TNG "The Big Goodbye"

1944 Nazi version of Brooklyn, New York City
ENT "Storm Front"

1950s Sisko's vision of New York City
DS9 "Far Beyond the Stars"

1957 Pittsburgh
ENT "Carbon Creek"

2000-2001 Portage Creek, Indiana
VGR "11:59"

2004 Carpenter Street, Detroit
ENT "Carpenter Street"

2153 San Francisco
ENT "The Expanse"

2372 New Orleans
DS9 "Homefront"

2372 Alternate Reality version of San Francisco
VGR "Non Sequitur"

EASTER EGGS AND IN-JOKES

The production team on *Star Trek* often had fun and hid in-jokes and Easter eggs in the displays, graphics, and even names on the different series. Most couldn't be found unless viewers froze the frame while watching an episode, but sometimes they were obvious. Some of the most fun include:

U.S.S. ENTERPRISE

GALAXY CLASS • STARFLEET REGISTRY NCC-1701-D
UTOPIA PLANITIA FLEET YARDS, MARS
FIFTH STARSHIP TO BEAR THE NAME • LAUNCHED STARDATE 40759.5
UNITED FEDERATION OF PLANETS

STARFLEET COMMAND	ENGINEERING GROUP	WARP TECHNOLOGIES DEVELOPMENT GROUP	ADVANCED TECHNOLOGIES UNIT
Adm. Gene Roddenberry	Capt. Andrew Probert	Capt. Robert Legato	Dr. Rick Sternbach
Adm. Rick Berman	Capt. Herman Zimmerman	Capt. Daniel Curry	Dr. Michael Okuda
Adm. Michael Piller	Capt. Richard James	Capt. Gary Hutzel	
Adm. David Livingston	Capt. John M. Dwyer	Capt. Ronald B. Moore	YARD ENGINEERS
Adm. Robert H. Justman	Capt. Jim Mees	Capt. Wendy Neuss	Capt. Gregory Jein
Adm. Peter Lauritson	Capt. Cari L. Thomas	Capt. Richard Arnold	Capt. Dana White
Adm. Susan Sackett	Capt. Richard McKenzie		

"...to boldly go where no one has gone before."

Dedication Plaques Every bridge on a Starfleet vessel includes a dedication plaque with a meaningful quote and a list of officers that had worked on the development of that particular ship. In reality, since the days of *The Next Generation* the "officers" listed are comprised of names in the production staff, with Gene Roddenberry serving as either "Admiral" or "Chief of Staff."

GNDN The sets of conduits and electrical relays in The Original Series were labeled to give the appearance of what an engineer needed to test or track down. Over time, GNDN began to appear in many places, a joke among the production crew that a particular pipe "goes nowhere, does nothing."

Tasha's Good-bye Wave Tasha Yar died in TNG's "Skin of Evil," making it a little prescient that Tasha Yar can be seen waving to the camera after Picard and Crusher leave a cargo hold in the episode that precedes it, "Symbiosis."

M*A*S*H-Up The character of Dr. Timicin in the TNG episode "Half a Life" was played by David Ogden Stiers. The noted actor is perhaps best known for his role of Major Charles Winchester on *M*A*S*H*, in which he was a member of the 4077th Mobile Army Surgical Hospital. A sensor analysis of Timicin's device in the episode reads 4077.

Hand of Apollo In *Star Trek Beyond*, Scotty mentioned several rumors surrounding the disappearance of the *U.S.S. Franklin*. One of those was that it encountered a "giant green hand," which was a callback to the *U.S.S. Enterprise*'s encounter with Apollo in the TOS episode "Who Mourns for Adonais?" The end credits for *Beyond* also showed an almost hand-shaped green nebula.

Promenade Directory When the production team designed the directory on Deep Space 9's Promenade, in-jokes were available in almost every store. Many science-fiction properties were name-dropped, from Spacely Sprockets (where George Jetson worked in *The Jetsons*); to Tom Servo's Used Robots (a reference to the *Mystery Science Theater 3000* hosts); to Yoyodyne Propulsion Systems (an homage to *The Adventures of Buckaroo Banzai Across the Eighth Dimension!*). Production staff also had some floor space: executive producer Rick Berman apparently sold dilithium at Berman's Dilithium Supply and production designer Herman Zimmerman had his own restaurant, Chez Zimmerman.

The Tribble Factor Two Starfleet temporal agents interrogated Sisko about his crew's trip back in time to Space Station K-7 and his interactions on the *U.S.S. Enterprise*. The investigators were named Luscly and Dulmur, which were anagrams for two other investigators of weird phenomena Scully and Mulder of the television show *The X-Files*.

DS9 "TRIALS AND TRIBBLE-ATIONS"

What Eugenics Wars? When the *Voyager* crew went back in time to 1996 Earth, they found no trace of the Eugenics Wars. However, astronomer Rain Robinson had not only a model of the *S.S. Botany Bay* in her office, but an action figure of a Talosian.

VGR "FUTURE'S END"

Scotty's Memories While Scotty only felt like a relic during his time aboard the *Enterprise*-D, the appearance of a cast member from The Original Series was a chance to pepper homages into the script. He referenced events from "The Naked Time," "Wolf in the Fold," and "Elaan of Troyius," and drank a "green beverage," a callback to "By Any Other Name." He left the *Enterprise*-D in the shuttle Justman, named for TOS producer Robert Justman.

TNG "RELICS"

ALL IN THE FAMILY

GENE RODDENBERRY'S WIFE MAJEL WAS OFTEN KNOWN AS THE FIRST LADY OF *STAR TREK* NOT ONLY BECAUSE SHE WAS MARRIED TO GENE, BUT BECAUSE SHE PLAYED MANY ROLES IN THE DIFFERENT SERIES OVER THE YEARS. ONE OF THE MORE NOTABLE ROLES CAME DURING *THE NEXT GENERATION* AS SHE TOOK ON THE PART OF DEANNA TROI'S MOTHER, AND ASSUMED A NEW UNOFFICIAL TITLE AS "AUNTIE MAME OF THE GALAXY." BUT THE WIFE OF *STAR TREK*'S CREATOR IS NOT THE ONLY MEMBER OF THE EXTENDED FAMILY OF ACTORS AND PRODUCTION PERSONNEL TO APPEAR. MANY OTHER *STAR TREK* ACTORS HAVE ALSO HAD RELATIVES BEAM ON BOARD TO PLAY ROLES.

John Billingsley's wife Bonita Friedericy played a scientist turned Borg in the *Enterprise* episode "Regeneration."

Chris Pine's father Robert Pine played alien ambassador Liria in the *Voyager* episode "The Chute" and Vulcan captain Tavin in the *Enterprise* episode "Fusion" several years before his son took the role of Captain Kirk in the *Kelvin* Timeline films.

Wil Wheaton's sister Amy Wheaton played an uncredited role in *The Next Generation* episode "When The Bough Breaks."

William Shatner's daughters Two of Shatner's daughters, Lisabeth and Leslie, played children in The Original Series episode "Miri." His daughter Melanie later played a yeoman in *Star Trek: The Final Frontier*.

James Doohan's twin sons Christopher and Montgomery Doohan were extras in *Star Trek: The Motion Picture* and Christopher played a transporter technician in *Star Trek Into Darkness*.

Patrick Stewart's son Daniel Stewart played Batai, Kamin's (Patrick Stewart's) son in the TNG episode "The Inner Light."

John de Lancie's son Keegan de Lancie played Q's (John de Lancie's) son in the "Q2" episode of *Voyager*.

Acting is a job unlike any other. Producers and casting directors of TV shows like to hire people they can rely on, especially with weekly deadlines looming. Actors already familiar with the elaborate makeup and technobabble terms in *Star Trek* are an additional bonus. It's no surprise that numerous familiar faces turned up occasionally across the series in the franchise.

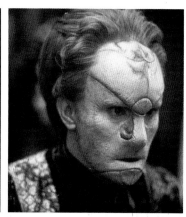

Jeffrey Combs

- **Brunt** DS9 Multiple episodes
- **Weyoun (Multiple versions)** DS9 Multiple episodes
- **Tiron** DS9 "Meridian"
- **Shran** ENT Multiple episodes
- **Krem** ENT "Acquisition"
- **Penk** VGR "Tsunkatse"
- **Kevin Mulkahey** DS9 "Far Beyond the Stars"
- **Holosuite Guest** DS9 "What You Leave Behind"

J.G. Hertzler

- **Vulcan Captain** DS9 "Emissary"
- **Martok** DS9 Multiple episodes
- **Laas** DS9 "Chimera"
- **Holosuite Guest** DS9 "What You Leave Behind"
- **Hirogen fighter** VGR "Tsunkatse"
- **Kolos** ENT "Judgment"
- **Klingon Commander** ENT "Borderland"
- **Roy Rittenhouse** DS9 "Far Beyond the Stars"

Thomas Kopache

- **Mirok** TNG "The Next Phase"
- **Train engineer** TNG "Emergence"
- **Communications Officer** *Star Trek Generations*
- **Kira Taban** DS9 Multiple episodes
- **Viorsa** VGR "The Thaw"
- **Tos** ENT "Broken Bow"
- **Test subject** ENT "Harbinger"

Randy Oglesby

- **Scholar** TNG "Loud as a Whisper"
- **Ah-Kel/Ro-Kel** DS9 "Vortex"
- **Silaran Prin** DS9 "The Darkness and the Light"
- **Kir** VGR "Counterpoint"

- **Trena'L** ENT "Unexpected"
- **Degra** ENT Multiple episodes

Vaughn Armstrong

Holds the record for playing the most separate *Star Trek* characters.

- **Korris** TNG Multiple episodes
- **Danar** DS9 "Past Prologue"
- **Seskal** DS9 Multiple episodes
- **Telek R'Mor** VGR "Eye of the Needle"
- **Lansor (Two of Nine)** VGR "Survival Instinct"
- **Vidiian Captain** VGR "Fury"

- **Alpha Hirogen** VGR "Flesh and Blood"
- **Korath** VGR "Endgame"
- **Klingon Captain** ENT "Sleeping Dogs"
- **Kreetassan leader** ENT Multiple episodes
- **Admiral Maxwell Forrest** ENT Multiple episodes

BEFORE THEY WERE FAMOUS

EVERYONE STARTS SOMEWHERE . . . AND MANY FAMOUS HOLLYWOOD ACTORS HAVE GONE ON TO EVEN GREATER FAME AFTER THEY GUEST-STARRED ON AN EPISODE OR *STAR TREK* FILM, INCLUDING:

Kirstie Alley The *Cheers* and *Fat Actress* star landed her first role as the poker-faced Saavik, Spock's protégé in *Star Trek II: The Wrath of Khan*.

Chris Hemsworth Before he ever lifted a hammer as the comic book thunder god, Thor, Hemsworth had the small but pivotal role in the rebooted *Star Trek* film franchise. Briefly the captain of the *U.S.S. Kelvin*, George Kirk sacrificed himself to save his wife and newborn son, James T. Kirk.

STAR TREK (2009)

Joan Collins Before she was the grande dame of *Dynasty*, the future Mrs. Alexis Carrington was the time-crossed love of James T. Kirk, social worker and peace activist Edith Keeler.

TOS "THE CITY ON THE EDGE OF FOREVER"

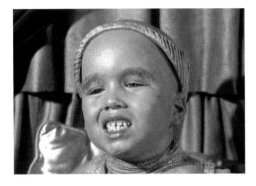

Terri Garr Before she became a regular in Mel Brooks's comedies such as *Young Frankenstein* and *High Anxiety*, Terri played Gary Seven's assistant, Roberta Lincoln. Their episode was meant to be a "backdoor pilot" for a new show that never came to pass.

TOS "ASSIGNMENT: EARTH"

Clint Howard Superstar director Ron Howard was already playing Opie on the *Andy Griffith Show* when his little brother, Clint, started his own acting career. The future (insert many films here) star made a big splash as the little alien Balok.

TOS "THE CORBOMITE MANEUVER"

Teri Hatcher Before her roles as a desperate housewife or Lois Lane, Teri Hatcher guest-starred in an episode of *The Next Generation* as a transporter officer (and date) of the outrageous Okona.

TNG "THE OUTRAGEOUS OKONA"

Ashley Judd Daughter and sister to the country music legends the Judds, Ashley became famous as an actress in films such as *Double Jeopardy* and *Divine Secrets of the Ya-Ya Sisterhood* after she caught the eye of Ensign Wesley Crusher as Lieutenant Robin Lefler.

TNG "THE GAME"

Kirsten Dunst Eventually Dunst would *Bring It On* as a head cheerleader and play Mary Jane Watson in the Tobey Maguire *Spider-Man* films. One of her first jobs was Hedril, the telepathic Cairn child that triggered Lwaxana's painful repressed memories of her first daughter who died tragically.

TNG "DARK PAGE"

Dwayne "The Rock" Johnson By the time Dwayne Johnson appeared on *Voyager* as a tsunkatse fighter, most of the world knew him as "the Rock." Still, Johnson had other things cooking, and his guest appearance on *Voyager* led to a movie career that is still going strong.

VGR "TSUNKATSE"

Kim Cattrall Before Samantha Jones opened a PR firm in New York and began hanging out with the other girls in *Sex and the City*, Kim Cattrall was no stranger to films, having been in the original *Porky's*. However, *Star Trek* fans know her best for Spock's second Vulcan protégé, the traitorous Valeris.

STAR TREK VI: THE UNDISCOVERED COUNTRY

Sarah Silverman Comedian Sarah Silverman would one day have her own television show and become an outspoken activist, but early on she guest-starred as astronomer Rain Robinson in a two-part *Star Trek: Voyager* story where she helped the crew avert a temporal crisis.

VGR "FUTURE'S END"

Tom Hardy British stage actor Tom Hardy was hardly known to American audiences when he was cast as Shinzon, the Romulan clone of Captain Jean-Luc Picard, but Hardy's star continued to rise and he was nominated for an Oscar in 2015's *The Revenant*.

STAR TREK NEMESIS

In Hollywood, a cameo appearance is simply a guest role that a famous actor takes in a show or film to help boost ratings for a series, or to add buzz to a film. With *Star Trek*, so many actors are fans of the show that they often ask to be in an episode or film simply for the fun of it.

Ray Walston Walston played the lovable Uncle Martin in the1960s sitcom *My Favorite Martian*, along with many other roles before taking on the part of the wise and enigmatic Boothby to advise a number of Starfleet cadets.

TNG "THE FIRST DUTY"/
VGR "IN THE FLESH"/"THE FIGHT"

Whoopi Goldberg A fan of The Original Series, Oscar-winner Goldberg asked her friend LeVar Burton to get her a part on *The Next Generation*. Her role of Guinan the bartender grew over the years, and the cameo became a recurring part that extended even to *The Next Generation* films.

TNG

Ben Vereen Tony-award winning singer and actor Vereen played Geordi La Forge's father, Edward, in the episode "Interface." Years before, Burton had played Vereen's grandfather in the acclaimed miniseries *Roots*.

TNG "INTERFACE"

Vanessa Williams The former Miss America and pop singer was a natural to be cast as Arandis, the facilitator for the Temtibi Lagoon on the pleasure planet, Risa.

DS9 "LET HE WHO IS WITHOUT SIN"

John Rhys-Davies Journeyman actor Rhys-Davies spent some time on the *Voyager* holodeck as Leonardo da Vinci, a mentor to Captain Janeway.

VGR "SCORPION"/"CONCERNING FLIGHT"

Jane Wiedlin Pop music and *Star Trek* crossed paths in *Star Trek IV: The Voyage Home* with a blink-and-you-might-miss-her appearance of Go-Go's guitarist Jane Wiedlin onscreen at Starfleet Command during the whale probe crisis.

STAR TREK IV: THE VOYAGE HOME

Ed Begley Jr. Actor Ed Begley Jr. is known for his role as Doctor Victor Erlich in the hit television show *St. Elsewhere*, as well as for his environmental advocacy. Thus, he was playing against type when cast as the temporal corporate magnate Henry Starling.

VGR "FUTURE'S END"

John Tesh Former *Entertainment Tonight* host and new-age music composer, Tesh documented his appearance on *The Next Generation* as a holographic Klingon that hit Worf with a painstik during a Klingon ritual.

TNG "THE ICARUS FACTOR"

Jason Alexander Famous for his role as the hapless George Costanza on *Seinfeld*, Alexander took on the character of Kurros, part of an alien think tank in the Delta Quadrant.

VGR "THINK TANK"

Mick Fleetwood Founding member of the legendary Fleetwood Mac appeared as an Antedean ambassador completely covered in fish-faced makeup.

TNG "MANHUNT"

Christian Slater The star of *Heathers* had a cameo as a night-duty officer who had to wake up Captain Sulu in *Star Trek VI: The Undiscovered Country*.

Seth MacFarlane The creator of the animated hits *Family Guy* and *American Dad* appeared in two episodes of *Star Trek: Enterprise* as Ensign Rivers.
ENT "THE FORGOTTEN"/"AFFLICTION"

Kelsey Grammer Frasier himself phoned in a performance in *The Next Generation* episode "Cause and Effect" as Captain Morgan Bateson of the *U.S.S. Bozeman*. Bebe Neuwirth, who played Frasier's ex-wife, Lilith, also beamed over to the planet Malcoria, as a scientist who helped (and flirted with) a captured Riker.
TNG "CAUSE AND EFFECT"/
"FIRST CONTACT"

James Worthy Los Angeles Lakers basketball legend James Worthy at 6'9" played the tallest Klingon, Koral, in *The Next Generation* episode "Gambit, Part II."

Abdullah bin Al-Hussein, King of Jordan He was still a prince at the time of his appearance, but the future king was excited to take on the role of a science officer aboard a Federation starship.
VGR "INVESTIGATIONS."

Iggy Pop The godfather of punk appeared as the Vorta Yelgrun in the DS9 episode "The Magnificent Ferengi."

PASSING THE TORCH

IN SUCH AN INTERTWINED UNIVERSE, IT'S NO SURPRISE THAT CHARACTERS FROM ONE *STAR TREK* SERIES MIGHT POP UP ON ANOTHER. IT ALSO DOESN'T HURT THE RATINGS. EVEN *VOYAGER*, 70,000 LIGHT-YEARS FROM HOME, MANAGED TO HAVE SOME FAVORITE CHARACTERS CROSS OVER TO SHARE SOME SCREEN TIME.

Admiral McCoy The elderly Admiral McCoy took a tour of the *U.S.S. Enterprise*-D before its launch, with Data as his guide.

TNG "ENCOUNTER AT FARPOINT"

Sarek/Spock The revered Vulcan ambassador showed up twice on *The Next Generation*. His emotionally crippling illness made him unable to complete a negotiation without mind-melding with Captain Picard. Picard then brought things full circle after Sarek's death and melded with Spock to let him experience the pride and love his father had not been able to previously express.

TNG "SAREK"/"UNIFICATION"

Scotty After being trapped in a transporter pattern buffer for 70 years, Scotty wondered if he had a place in the next generation of Starfleet. His teamwork with Geordi La Forge convinced him he was still a "miracle worker," and he left the ship with no plans to retire.

TNG "RELICS"

Picard While Commander Sisko blamed Captain Picard for his wife's death, Picard nevertheless showed up to discuss Sisko's assignment as commander of Deep Space 9.

DS9 "EMISSARY"

Kor, Kang, and Koloth *Deep Space Nine* had three Klingons from The Original Series band together with Dax to seek vengeance on the man who killed their firstborn sons.

DS9 "BLOOD OATH"

Janeway Promoted to admiral after her return from the Delta Quadrant, Janeway ordered Captain Picard to head to Romulus at the invitation of the new praetor.

STAR TREK NEMESIS

EMH During *Star Trek: First Contact*, Dr. Crusher overcame her distaste for the Emergency Medical Hologram and used it to stall the Borg so she could evacuate the sickbay on the *Enterprise*-E.

STAR TREK: FIRST CONTACT

The Original Series Crew The Deep Space 9 officers were involved in a time-travel incident where they went back in time and found themselves involved in the events of the original series episode "The Trouble with Tribbles."

DS9 "TRIALS AND TRIBBLE-ATIONS"

Riker Will Riker (or reasonable facsimiles) crossed over to other shows often. His transporter double, Tom Riker, posed as him to steal the *U.S.S. Defiant*. Later, Q pulled him into the Delta Quadrant for a trial of another Q. Finally, Riker and Counselor Troi interacted with holographic representations of the crew of *Enterprise* NX-01.

*DS9 "DEFIANT"/VGR "DEATH WISH"/
ENT "THESE ARE THE VOYAGES . . ."*

Barclay/Troi Reginald Barclay was instrumental in establishing communications with *Voyager* and, along with some emotional assistance from Counselor Deanna Troi, was an important link between the crew and the Federation.

VGR "PATHFINDER"/"LIFE LINE"

Chekov/Scotty/Kirk The maiden voyage of the *Enterprise*-B brought out veterans of the first ship to bear the name: Captains Kirk, Scott, and Chekov. Disaster struck and the last anyone saw of Captain James T. Kirk was when he left the bridge to save the ship. He reappeared in the Nexus, where a century later he would encounter Captain Picard and save an entire planet in his last heroic act.

STAR TREK GENERATIONS

Quark Though cut from the film *Star Trek: Insurrection*, a scene on the DVD extras revealed that Quark planned to open up businesses on the Ba'ku planet, before being unceremoniously stopped.

STAR TREK: INSURRECTION

Spock An accidental trip back through time after a red matter explosion helped create the *Kelvin* Timeline, allowing Spock from the Prime universe to interact with younger versions of Kirk and himself.

STAR TREK/STAR TREK INTO DARKNESS

Before the advent of more affordable CGI, once a starship or space station was designed and the model built, the *Star Trek* production staff would repaint or revise the detailing on it to reuse it multiple times for different alien species.

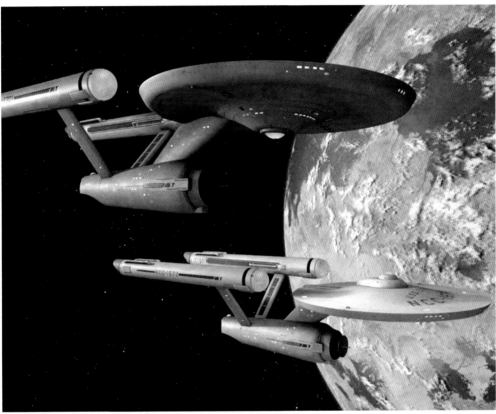

U.S.S. Enterprise The most obvious use of recycled ship models occurred with Federation vessels, and specifically the *U.S.S. Enterprise* NCC-1701. It was only logical for Starfleet to have certain classes of ships built to the same specifications. By establishing this practice, producers were able to use the *Enterprise* shooting model as the standard for all *Constitution*-class vessels by just changing out the registry numbers on the primary hull. The familiar ship became the *Constellation*, *Defiant*, *Hood*, and *Potemkin* among others, and it continued to stick with that established design with the digital remastering of the series and future shows that relied on CGI as well.

S.S. Botany Bay Khan's ship from "Space Seed" was also the doomed *Woden* in "The Ultimate Computer." TOS

Tholian ship This triangular ship from "The Tholian Web" was refurbished to be the *Aurora* in "The Way to Eden." TOS

Orbital office complex What began as a Starfleet office station in *Star Trek: The Motion Picture* was turned upside down and became Regula I in *Star Trek II: The Wrath of Khan*. It was also used as other starbases in TNG and a prison in DS9.

Talarian warship The Talarian design was refurbished several times as a Kriosian ship, a Drayan shuttle, a Frunalian vessel, and the *Sherval Das*. TNG "Suddenly Human"/"The Perfect Mate"/DS9 "Emissary"/"Sons of Mogh"/VGR "Innocence"

Amargosa Observatory The observatory in *Generations* took on new life as the wormhole relay station in the DS9 episode "Destiny."

Mercenary ship The ship that bore Valkris to Kruge so she could deliver him the information on Genesis in *Star Trek III: The Search for Spock* was modified to be vessels in both TNG and DS9 as well as the Vidiian starship in the *Voyager* episode "Phage."

Batris The freighter commandeered by Klingons in the TNG episode "Heart of Glory" appeared in numerous TNG, DS9, and VGR episodes including: TNG "Symbiosis"/"Unification"/DS9 "The Passenger"/VGR "The Chute"

Nenebek The small ship was remodeled several times from its first appearance in *The Next Generation* episode "The Most Toys," becoming a time pod as well as shuttles for the J'naii, Yridians, and Iyarans. TNG "A Matter of Time"/"The Outcast"/"Birthright"/ "Liaisons"

U.S.S. Reliant While many ships of the same class could easily be modified by simply changing the name and registry number, the *Reliant* from *Star Trek II: The Wrath of Khan* also doubled as the *U.S.S. Bozeman* in TNG's "Cause and Effect," after some modifications.

Talarian observation craft Talarian ships had a versatile design, as this was also remodeled to be another Kriosian ship, a Tamarian cruiser, a Bothan ship, and a T'Lani cruiser. TNG "Suddenly Human"/"The Perfect Mate"/"Darmok"/DS9 "Armageddon Game"/VGR "Persistence of Vision"

Husnock warship Perhaps the most versatile model of all, the Husnock ship from the TNG episode "The Survivors" became over twenty different ships among the TNG, DS9, VGR, and ENT series.

REDRESSED

While some of the fashions on *Star Trek* are certainly otherworldly, sometimes the wardrobe staff would have to "make it work" and repurpose old outfits for new aliens or simply reuse the entire garment. Of special note is that Garak's tailor shop on Deep Space 9 stocked a lot of old costumes from *The Next Generation*.

Andorian vest Thelev's triangular vest worn in "Journey to Babel" ended up on a prisoner in "Whom Gods Destroy." TOS

Pink shirt and white dress Two off-duty crew women in different eras wore the same pink shirt and white dress in "The Cage" and "Where No Man Has Gone Before." TOS

Eminiar VII hats The triangular and squared hats of the people of Eminiar VII in "A Taste of Armageddon" show up on prisoners in "Whom Gods Destroy." TOS

Police security uniforms The Rutians, Vulcans, Mari, and others have all used the same uniform with some differences in TNG "The Higher Ground," DS9 "Vortex," and VGR "Random Thoughts."

Zalkonian military This uniform from the TNG episode "Transfigurations" was adopted by the Dopterians in DS9's "The Way of the Warrior."

Dr. Wallace Her pink and gold dress from "The Deadly Years" was also seen on a woman in the Starnes Expedition in "And the Children Shall Lead" TOS

Yareena's jumpsuit After Yareena's fight in the TNG episode "Code of Honor," her jumpsuit was later seen on someone in Ten-Forward as well as Garak's Clothiers. DS9 "Sanctuary"

Sovak's colorful shirt The Ferengi equivalent of a Hawaiian shirt showed up first in the TNG episode "Captain's Holiday," then in Garak's shop where Nog ended up with it. DS9 "Sanctuary"

Green & yellow rose dress Perhaps the most ubiquitous fashion statement in *Star Trek*, the dress appears numerous times in *Deep Space Nine*, two movies (*Generations* and *Nemesis*), *Voyager* and *Enterprise*. DS9 "Rivals"/ VGR "Drive"/ENT "Terra Prime"

REMADE

MAKING A TELEVISION EPISODE EACH WEEK CAN GET COSTLY, ESPECIALLY WHEN IT IS SET IN OUTER SPACE IN A FUTURE WITH NEW TECHNOLOGY. THE PRODUCERS OF *STAR TREK* MANAGED TO COME IN ON BUDGET BY REUSING PROPS OR PARTS OF PROPS TO CREATE SOMETHING FOR A NEW EPISODE. THESE ARE JUST SOME OF THE PROPS THAT MADE MULTIPLE APPEARANCES IN THE FRANCHISE:

 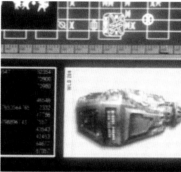 

Exocomp The sentient robots from "The Quality of Life" (TNG) lived again as three devices in *Star Trek: Enterprise*, including a Xindi machine in "Anomaly."

Nomad Parts of the space probe from "The Changeling" were repurposed to be both the M-4 in "Requiem for Methuselah" and the Romulan cloaking device in "The *Enterprise* Incident." TOS

Artificial intelligence The machine member of the *Voyager* "Think Tank" episode was also a photonic field generator in "Flesh and Blood," and a mining device in the *Enterprise* episode "Civilization."

Trill device Odan the Trill ambassador used this unknown device once in TNG's "The Host." It later became another type of dermal regenerator in DS9 episodes like "One Little Ship."

Engineering scanner This device from "Samaritan Snare" and "Peak Performance" ended up as a hair-styling tool in "Data's Day." TNG

Dermal regenerator The dermal regenerator seen in "Chain of Command" and "Timescape" did triple duty as an engineering scanner Geordi used on Data's head in "Time's Arrow," a subdermal scalpel in "Latent Image," and a microinducer in "Scientific Method." TNG/VGR

Dome The glass dome of Lazarus's shuttle in "The Alternative Factor" also housed the glowing brains of the Providers in "The Gamesters of Triskelion." TOS

SCM model 3 Wesley's superconducting magnet model 3 that he showed off in "The Dauphin" (TNG) showed up in the hand of one of the solanogen-based aliens from "Schisms" (TNG) and as the trajectory matrix in "Prime Factors" (VGR).

Microcellular scanner This scanner changed functions from a medical scanner to an engineering device during the run of *Deep Space Nine*.

Kivas Fajo's forcefield device This gadget became a medical device in Dr. Crusher's hands in TNG, used for everything from treating cuts to torn ligaments. It later became an engineering tool for B'Elanna Torres on *Voyager*.

Chapter 7

BY THE NUMBERS

As long as *Star Trek* endures, fans and critics will debate the merits of which episode was best overall, which episode was best in a certain series, or which episode might have been the best given current special effects technology. On website after website and at convention after convention (especially during the fiftieth Anniversary convention in 2016), certain episodes pop up again and again as the cream of the crop. Feel free to disagree.

TOS

"The City on the Edge of Forever"
"Where No Man Has Gone Before"
"Amok Time"
"Mirror, Mirror"
"The Trouble with Tribbles"

TAS

"Yesteryear"
"Mudd's Passion"
"The Lorelei Signal"

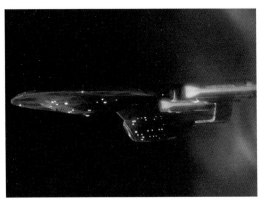

TNG

"Yesterday's *Enterprise*"
"Unification"
"The Inner Light"
"The Best of Both Worlds"
"All Good Things. . ."

DS9

"In the Pale Moonlight"
"Duet"
"It's Only a Paper Moon"
"The Visitor"
"Far Beyond the Stars"

VGR

"Year of Hell"
"Scorpion"
"Endgame"
"Timeless"
"Equinox"

ENT

"In a Mirror, Darkly"
"Similitude"
"The Andorian Incident"
"Carbon Creak"
"Demon/Terra Prime"

OPENING DAY

THE FILM INDUSTRY IS DEEPLY FOCUSED ON A MOVIE'S OPENING WEEKEND AND HOW MUCH MONEY THE FILM MAKES DURING ITS FIRST FEW DAYS OUT ON THE MARKET. THE HIGHLY ANTICIPATED REBOOT OF THE FRANCHISE IN 2009 REMAINS THE TOP OPENING WEEKEND FOR THE SERIES TO DATE, ESPECIALLY AS WORLDWIDE AUDIENCES—AND MOVIE PRICES—HAVE GROWN SINCE THE FIRST FILM RELEASED IN 1979. (THESE ARE RAW NUMBERS, NOT ADJUSTED FOR INFLATION. SOURCE: BOXOFFICEMOJO.COM)

Star Trek: The Motion Picture $11,926,421

Star Trek II: The Wrath of Khan $14,347,221

Star Trek III: The Search for Spock $16,673,295

Star Trek IV: The Voyage Home $16,688,888

Star Trek V: The Final Frontier $17,375,648

Star Trek VI: The Undiscovered Country $18,162,837

Star Trek Nemesis $18,513,305

Star Trek: Insurrection $22,052,836

Star Trek Generations $23,116, 394

Star Trek: First Contact $30,716,131

Star Trek Beyond $59,253,211

Star Trek Into Darkness $70,165,559

Star Trek (2009) $75,204,289

"HE'S DEAD, JIM."

MUCH LIKE DR. MCCOY'S OTHER CATCHPHRASE, "I'M A DOCTOR, NOT A . . .," THE TIMES MCCOY ACTUALLY SAID HIS SECOND-MOST QUOTABLE LINE IS FAR LESS THAN PEOPLE THINK. HE ONLY SAID THE FULL PHRASE "HE'S (OR SHE'S) DEAD, JIM" A TOTAL OF SIX TIMES IN THE ORIGINAL SERIES.

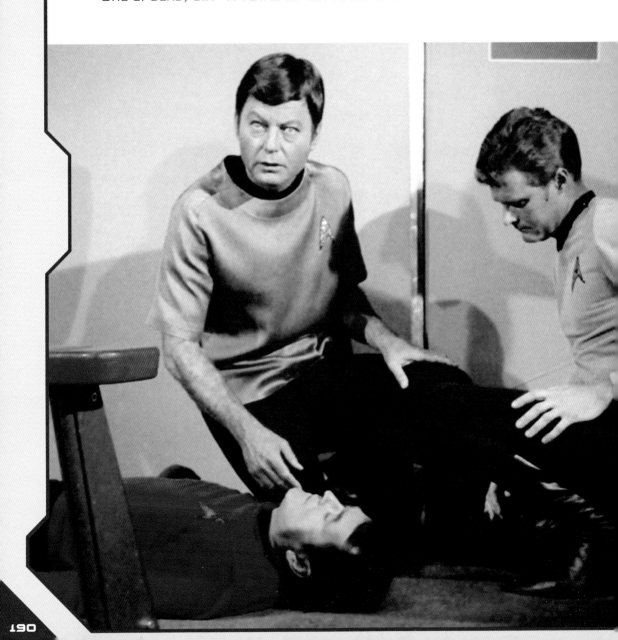

The dog from Alfa 177 "The Enemy Within"

Scotty (He got better) "The Changeling"

Kara, Sybo, and Hengist (A busy day for Dr. McCoy) "Wolf in the Fold"

Larry Marvick "Is There in Truth No Beauty?"

He varied his declarations twice with a "He's dead, Captain."

Professor Starnes "And the Children Shall Lead"

Tristan Adams "Dagger of the Mind"

And the rest of the time, it was a simple "He/she/it's dead."

Sturgeon "The Man Trap"

Teen boy "Miri"

Kirk (But not really.) "Amok Time"

Arlene Galway "The Deadly Years"

Nona "A Private Little War"

Chekov (Again, he got better.) "Spectre of the Gun"

Kirk/Sargon "Return to Tomorrow"

Old Man "For the World Is Hollow and I Have Touched the Sky"

TIMES
TIME TRAVEL

THE CREWS OF *STAR TREK* OFTEN ENDED UP TRAVELING BACKWARD OR FORWARDS IN TIME, FROZEN IN TIME, OR REPEATING MOMENTS OF TIME OVER AND OVER AGAIN. HOW MANY TIMES? FIFTY-ONE (INCLUDING ENCOUNTERS WITH SOME TEMPORAL ANOMALIES).

TOS

- "The Naked Time"
- "The City on the Edge of Forever"
- "All Our Yesterdays"
- "Assignment: Earth"
- "Tomorrow Is Yesterday"

TAS

- "Yesteryear"

TNG

- "All Good Things..."
- "Captain's Holiday"
- "Cause and Effect"
- "Firstborn"
- "Tapestry"
- "Time Squared"
- "Yesterday's Enterprise"
- "Time's Arrow"
- "A Matter of Time"
- "We'll Always Have Paris" (Temporal anomaly)
- "Timescape" (Temporal anomaly)

DS9

- "Accession"
- "Children of Time"
- "Little Green Men"
- "The Sound of Her Voice"
- "Past Tense"
- "Visionary"
- "The Visitor"
- "Trials and Tribble-ations"
- "Wrongs Darker Than Death or Night"
- "Time's Orphan"

VGR

- "Before and After"
- "Parallax"
- "Time and Again"
- "Death Wish"
- "Endgame"
- "Eye of the Needle"
- "Future's End"
- "Fury"
- "Timeless"
- "Relativity"
- "Non Sequitur" (Temporal anomaly)
- "Shattered" (Temporal anomaly)

ENT

- "Azati Prime"
- "Carpenter Street"
- "Cold Front"
- "E²"
- "Future Tense"
- "Shockwave"
- "Storm Front"
- "Zero Hour"

Films

- *Star Trek IV: The Voyage Home*
- *Star Trek Generations*
- *Star Trek: First Contact*
- *Star Trek* (2009)

ALONG WITH TIME TRAVEL, ONE OF THE COSMIC PHENOMENON *STAR TREK* CREWS ENCOUNTERED THE MOST WERE PARALLEL UNIVERSES OR ALTERNATE REALITIES. THESE REALITIES OCCURRED WHEREIN EVENTS, PLACES, AND PEOPLE WERE SIMILAR WITH SOME STARK DIFFERENCES. WHAT BECAME KNOWN AS THE "MIRROR UNIVERSE" WAS ONE OF THE MOST FAMOUS ALTERNATE REALITIES IN SCIENCE-FICTION HISTORY.

Lazarus's negative universe TOS "The Alternative Factor"

Reverse universe TAS "The Counter-Clock Incident"

Collapsed warp bubble TNG "Remember Me"

Multiple quantum universes TNG "Parallels"

***Kelvin* Timeline** *Star Trek* (2009)

The famed "Mirror Universe" shows up quite a bit in three different series.

TOS

"Mirror, Mirror"

"The Tholian Web" (unknown to be the Mirror Universe at the time)

DS9

"Crossover"

"Through the Looking Glass"

"Shattered Mirror"

"Resurrection"

"The Emperor's New Cloak"

ENT

"In a Mirror, Darkly"

Lazarus's negative universe TOS "The Alternative Factor"

Reverse universe TAS "The Counter-Clock Incident"

Collapsed warp bubble TNG "Remember Me"

Multiple quantum universes TNG "Parallels"

***Kelvin* Timeline** *Star Trek* (2009)

The famed "Mirror Universe" shows up quite a bit in three different series.

TOS

"Mirror, Mirror"

"The Tholian Web" (unknown to be the Mirror Universe at the time)

DS9

"Crossover"

"Through the Looking Glass"

"Shattered Mirror"

"Resurrection"

"The Emperor's New Cloak"

ENT

"In a Mirror, Darkly"

LIST #89 / DÉJÀ VU ALL OVER AGAIN

FEEL LIKE YOU'VE SEEN THAT SECURITY GUARD OR HELMSMAN BEFORE? SOME ACTORS SHOWED UP NUMEROUS TIMES ACROSS MULTIPLE SERIES— SOMETIMES IN DIFFERENT ROLES, SOMETIMES IN THE SAME ROLE. THE PERSON YOU'VE SEEN MOST, HOWEVER, MAY SURPRISE YOU. OR NOT.

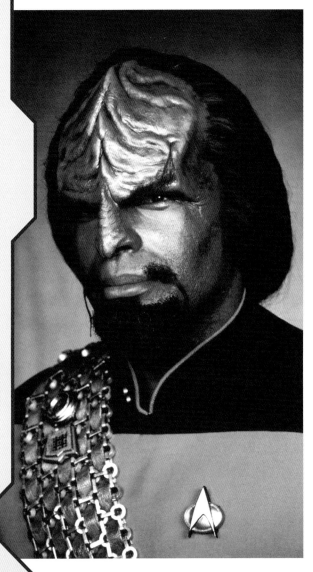

Michael Dorn Worf from *The Next Generation* appeared in almost every TNG episode, missing only two. He then went on to appear in 102 episode of *Deep Space Nine* and five of the *Star Trek* films, once portraying his ancestor in *Star Trek VI: The Undiscovered Country*.

James Doohan The actor best known as Scotty might not have been seen on screen more often than his fellow cast mates, but his voice definitely got a workout. Doohan provided voices for multiple characters in The Original Series, including Sargon in "Return to Tomorrow," the M-5 computer in "The Ultimate Computer," and the Oracle in "For the World Is Hollow and I Have Touched the Sky." Doohan's voice work really shined in *The Animated Series* where, in addition to voicing his most famous character, he also played fifty other parts.

Billy Blackburn DeForest Kelly's stand-in was also the uncredited Lieutenant Hadley for sixty-seven episodes of The Original Series.

Roger Holloway William Shatner's stand-in played the uncredited Lieutenant Lemli thirty-four times.

Michael Braveheart Braveheart played Crewman Martinez in 84 episodes of *The Next Generation* and *Star Trek: First Contact* as well as Klingons in *Voyager* and *Enterprise*.

Lorine Mendell Gates McFadden's stand-in also played the uncredited Crewman Diana Giddings in fifty-nine episodes.

Frank daVinci Leonard Nimoy's stand-in also played a number of uncredited extra roles in fifty-three episodes of The Original Series including Lieutenant Brent, Transporter Operator, Vulcan Ceremonial Aide, Eminiar Guard, and Security Guard.

Tracee Cocco A stuntwoman on TNG, she also played the uncredited Ensign Jae in sixty-three episodes, as well as a Borg drone. She also played several aliens in *Voyager*.

Barbara Babcock Not only did Babcock play Mea 3 and Philana on screen, she was the voice of a Tholian, a Zetaran, the Beta 5 computer, Trelane's mother, and Isis the cat.

TOS "A TASTE OF ARMAGGEDON"/
"PLATO'S STEPCHILDREN"/"THE THOLIAN WEB"/
"THE SQUIRE OF GOTHOS"/"ASSIGNMENT: EARTH"

Majel Barrett The actress who went on to marry Gene Roddenberry played Number One in the original pilot, Nurse Christine Chapel in thirty-six episodes of The Original Series (and two films), and various characters including Lieutenant M'Ress in *The Animated Series*. She later cemented her role as "The First Lady of *Star Trek*" by playing Deanna Troi's mother, Lwaxana, and the computer voices in TNG, DS9 and ENT.

FROM GOTHAM TO THE GALAXY

Campy and bright, the 1966 television version of *Batman* was far more of a comic-book romp than the superhero television shows and films of today. A number of actors, including a few who played some of *Batman*'s iconic villains, also showed off their acting chops on *Star Trek*.

Frank Gorshin The actor who played maniacal super villain the Riddler also portrayed the political traitor-hunting Bele in "Let That Be Your Last Battlefield."

Julie Newmar The feline felon, Catwoman, in the first two seasons of *Batman* served as the pregnant Eleen in "Friday's Child."

Joan Collins She sang a deadly song to Batman as the Siren, and as Edith Keeler she entranced Captain Kirk into a doomed relationship in "The City on the Edge of Forever."

Roger C. Carmel His character created counterfeit stamps in Gotham City as Colonel Gumm and also tried to swindle miners and the *Enterprise* crew as Harry Mudd in "Mudd's Women" and "I, Mudd," and he lent his voice and likeness to the animated "Mudd's Passion."

Yvonne Craig The redheaded crime fighter, Batgirl, also played the insane Orion Marta in "Whom Gods Destroy."

Lee Meriwether The actress who took over the role of Catwoman in the 1966 *Batman* film played the deadly Losira in "That Which Survives."

Leslie Parrish She played henchwoman to two super villains—Penguin and Mr. Freeze—but caught Apollo's eye as archaeologist Lt. Carolyn Palamas in "Who Mourns for Adonais?"

Grace Lee Whitney Guest starring on *Batman* as King Tut's jilted girlfriend Neila, Whitney is better known for playing Yeoman Rand in the early episodes of The Original Series.

Malachi Throne He wore a False Face on *Batman* and provided the male voice of the Talosian Keeper, as well as spanning generations to play Commodore Mendez in The Original Series episode "The Menagerie" and Pardek in *The Next Generation*'s "Unification."

MISSION: IMPOSSIBLE FUTURE

THE CREW OF THE *STARSHIP ENTERPRISE* WASN'T THE ONLY CAST ON TELEVISION IN THE 1960S WITH A MISSION. THE IMF, OR IMPOSSIBLE MISSIONS FORCE, WAS A TEAM OF SECRET AGENTS WHO WORKED TO MAKE SURE AMERICA AND THE WORLD WERE SAFE—AT LEAST ON TELEVISION. CONVENIENTLY, THE TWO SHOWS FILMED ON THE SAME STUDIO LOT SO THE ACTORS DIDN'T NEED TO TRAVEL FAR BETWEEN SOUNDSTAGES.

Leonard Nimoy After *Star Trek* ended, the former Spock went on to play Andrew "the Great" Paris, a master of disguise. He was on the series for two seasons.

Ricardo Montalban After originating the role of Khan in *Star Trek*, the future lead of Fantasy Island appeared in the *M:I* episode "Snowball in Hell"

William Shatner The heroic captain played against type as a killer convinced he was reliving the day of his crime.

George Takei Around the time *Star Trek* began airing, Takei took a guest role of Roger Lee in the episode "The Carriers."

Mark Lenard A role on *M:I* as Aristo Skoro reunited the Sarek actor with his *Star Trek* "son," Leonard Nimoy, for an episode.

Michael Ansara *Star Trek* fans know him best as Kang in "Day of the Dove," but Ansara also played Ed Stoner in the *M:I* episode "The Western."

Vic Tayback Playing a criminal in *M:I* was a role Tayback had some experience with as he was previously Krako in the TOS episode "A Piece of the Action."

Arlene Martel Nimoy was also reunited with his Vulcan betrothed from "Amok Time" when Martel played Atheda in an episode of *M:I*.

Joan Collins Kirk's ill-fated love from "The City on the Edge of Forever" played the title character in the *M:I* episode "Nicole"

Malachi Throne The actor played Ambassador Brazneck in an episode of *M:I* and Commodore Mendez in "The Menagerie."

Barbara Luna The "captain's woman" from the Mirror Universe episode "Mirror, Mirror" played a sexy spy in an episode of *M:I*.

Simon Pegg More recently, the actor/screenwriter in the *Kelvin* Timeline *Star Trek* films has also appeared as Benji Dunn, an IMF field agent in the *Mission: Impossible* films starring Tom Cruise. Not coincidentally, these films, like the *Star Trek* movies, were also produced by J.J. Abrams.

LIST #92 / KOBAYASHI MARU

GIVEN THE GRIND OF PRODUCING A WEEKLY TELEVISION SHOW, IT'S DIFFICULT TO HAVE EVERY EPISODE A CRITICAL SUCCESS. SOME EPISODES OF *STAR TREK* ARE GENERALLY AGREED UPON AS SOME OF THE LEAST POPULAR IN MOST POLLS AMONG FANS. AGAIN, FEEL FREE TO DISAGREE.

Chapter 8

TO BOLDLY GO . . .

A Trek Through Pop Culture

LIST #93 / BIG TREK THEORY

SOME OF *STAR TREK*'S BIGGEST FANS HAVE BEEN TELEVISION CHARACTERS—THE FOUR GEEKY SCIENTISTS OF *THE BIG BANG THEORY*. THOUGH THEY ALL LOVE THE SERIES, THE CHARACTER OF SHELDON DOES HAVE AN ONGOING LOVE/HATE RIVALRY WITH ACTOR WIL WHEATON, WHO OCCASIONALLY GUEST-STARS AS HIMSELF. WHILE WILLIAM SHATNER (KIRK) HAS NOT APPEARED ON THE SHOW TO DATE, HE AND SERIES STAR KALEY CUOCO PORTRAYED FATHER AND DAUGHTER IN A NUMBER OF COMMERCIALS IN AN ADVERTISING CAMPAIGN. OTHER *STAR TREK* CROSSOVERS INCLUDE:

George Takei (Sulu) Appeared in Howard's bedroom fantasy, along with Katee Sackhoff (Starbuck from *Battlestar Galactica*) to give Howard advice on romancing Bernadette.

Brent Spiner (Data) Became Sheldon's mortal enemy when he opened an original mint-in-package Wesley Crusher action figure signed by his "close personal friend Wil Wheaton."

LeVar Burton (Geordi La Forge) After being invited to Sheldon's party, the actor quickly left when he walked in on Barry, Zack, and Stuart singing karaoke. He later guest-starred in two episodes of Sheldon's YouTube series "Sheldon Cooper Presents: Fun with Flags," the last time on the promise Sheldon would delete his contact information.

Leonard Nimoy (Spock) Voiced a Spock action figure that chided Sheldon for replacing his broken transporter toy with Leonard's toy.

Brian George (Richard Bashir/O'Zaal) The Antarian ambassador in *Star Trek: Voyager* and Julian Bashir's father in *Star Trek: Deep Space Nine* also plays the recurring role of Rajesh Koothrapali's father on *The Big Bang Theory*.

POPULAR PROSE

THE FIRST *STAR TREK* BOOKS WERE COLLECTIONS OF THE EPISODES TOLD IN A SHORT-STORY FORMAT, AND PUBLISHED BEGINNING IN 1967 BY BANTAM BOOKS. WHITMAN PUBLISHING RELEASED THE FIRST ORIGINAL *STAR TREK* PROSE NOVEL, WITH NOVELIZATIONS OF *THE ANIMATED SERIES* FOLLOWING, AS WELL AS BOOKS FOR YOUNGER READERS. WITH THE RELEASE OF *STAR TREK: THE MOTION PICTURE* IN 1979, POCKET BOOKS ACQUIRED THE LICENSE TO PUBLISH *STAR TREK* FICTION AND CONTINUES TO PRODUCE BOOKS BASED ON THE SHOWS. THESE ARE JUST A FEW OF THE NOTABLE NOVELS PUBLISHED OVER THE DECADES:

Mission to Horatius The first *Star Trek* fiction published, the *Enterprise* crew visits a system of three planets in various stages of development.

Federation The crews of The Original Series and *The Next Generation* must work together to rescue a kidnapped Zefram Cochrane before his warp technology is used to conquer the Galaxy.

Imzadi The love story between Commander Riker and Counselor Troi is explored in the past and a future in which Troi is wrongfully killed.

Spock Must Die! Echoing "The Enemy Within," Spock is duplicated in a transporter accident.

The Entropy Effect A former scientist turned madman kills Kirk, and Spock must travel back in time to save him.

A Stitch in Time Andrew Robinson, who played Garak on DS9, wrote this story exploring his character's past and his return to Cardassia after the Dominion war.

Enterprise, The First Adventure This novel features the story of James Kirk's first trip aboard the *Enterprise* before they began their historic five-year mission.

Mosaic *Voyager* co-creator Jeri Taylor wrote the definitive backstory of Captain Kathryn Janeway, which she followed up with *Pathways*.

The Eugenics Wars Greg Cox wrote the three-volume series of books chronicling the rise and fall of Kirk's greatest foe, Khan Noonien Singh.

Crossover A sequel to the episode "Unification," Spock is taken hostage and the *Enterprise*-D crew, along with 140-year-old Admiral McCoy and Captain Montgomery Scott, come to the rescue.

Dark Mirror Only the crew of the *Enterprise*-D never made an appearance in the Mirror Universe on television (even *Voyager* was represented by a mirror version of Tuvok). *Dark Mirror* brings the *Enterprise*-D face-to-face with its counterpart.

Star Trek: The Motion Picture This *Star Trek* film novelization is the only book that creator Gene Roddenberry ever wrote, and fills in much of the detail that didn't make it onscreen in the first film.

House of Cards (New Frontier #1) The first novels to feature a crew and ship not shown on television, New Frontier followed the adventures of Captain Mackenzie Calhoun and the *U.S.S. Excalibur*.

COLLECT THEM ALL

DURING ITS FIFTY-PLUS YEAR HISTORY, STAR TREK HAS ENJOYED A WIDE VARIETY OF MERCHANDISE THAT WAS OFFICIALLY SANCTIONED BY THE STUDIO. FROM TRADING CARDS TO ACTION FIGURES—EVEN A LAS VEGAS ATTRACTION—COMPANIES HAVE TRIED EVERYTHING UNDER THE ASTEROID BELT TO CREATE NEW AND DIFFERENT STAR TREK-THEMED COLLECTIBLES, INCLUDING SOME RATHER UNIQUE ITEMS.

Barbie and Ken For the thirtieth anniversary of *Star Trek*, Barbie and Ken got in on the action. A special display package held the famous couple, Barbie in a red operations uniform and Ken in command gold. For the fiftieth anniversary of The Original Series, Mattel took the line even further, creating a special series of dolls featuring Uhura, Kirk, Spock, and a limited-edition Orion woman (Vina) for San Diego Comic-Con.

Lottery Tickets In the mid-1990s, *Star Trek* lottery tickets featuring different starships were released in several states. More were released around the world in recent years.

Star Trek Cookbook Written by Neelix himself, Ethan Phillips, the cookbook featured twentieth-century Earth equivalents of famed *Star Trek* dishes, as well as recipes from some of the other actors, and a section of food as props from *Voyager*'s prop master.

Star Trek: The Experience When Las Vegas reinvented itself as a family-friendly destination in the late 1990s, it made perfect sense to add *Star Trek* to the mix. Located in the Las Vegas Hilton off the Strip, the 65,000 square foot attraction boasted museum displays of costumes and props from the shows and an interactive ride where passengers were "beamed" aboard the *Enterprise*-D and then put in a shuttle that was attacked by Klingons. The ride deposited passengers onto the Deep Space 9 Promenade next to Quark's Bar, where they could drink a Warp Core Breach with friends. The attraction closed in 2008.

Marshmallow Dispenser The campfire scene in *Star Trek V: The Final Frontier* inspired a marshmallow dispenser as a special mail-away premium from Kraft.

Slot Machines Despite having a themed attraction in Las Vegas, it wasn't until 2008 that official *Star Trek* slot machines hit town. The video slot machine featured bonus rounds including "Tribble Pinball" and has spawned additional *Star Trek* slot machines.

Star Trek Putty *Star Trek* putty and Mr. Spock adhesive stained-glass stickers were just two products that grew out of the licensing program for *Star Trek: The Motion Picture*.

Star Trek Metal Detector In case scanners were down, one could use this to find any lost phaser parts.

Fragrances Palm Beach Beauté created perfumes and colognes based on *Star Trek* including the scents *Pon farr*, Sulu, Tiberius, and Red Shirt.

Enterprise Pizza Cutters While this century may debate on whether thin or thick crust is the best pizza, future generations will debate on which starship cuts pizza best – the original *Enterprise* or the *Enterprise*-D. Think Geek created stainless steel pizza cutters shaped like both ships.

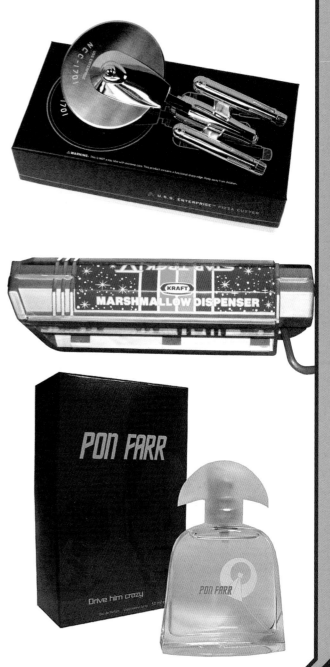

WARDROBE MALFUNCTION

PERHAPS THE ONLY MORE DANGEROUS THING TO BE THAN A RED-SHIRTED CREWMAN IN THE ORIGINAL SERIES WAS CAPTAIN KIRK'S SHIRT. IT WAS TORN OR COMPLETELY FORGOTTEN IN NUMEROUS EPISODES, TO THE POINT WHERE THE IDEA OF SHIRTLESS KIRK WAS EVEN PARODIED IN THE 1999 FILM GALAXY QUEST.

"Where No Man Has Gone Before"

"Charlie X"

"Court Martial"

"The Corbomite Maneuver"

"The Enemy Within"

"Journey to Babel"

"Patterns of Force"

"The Paradise Syndrome"

"The Empath"

"Shore Leave"

"Amok Time"

"Gamesters of Triskelion"

WHO SAID THAT?

As *Star Trek* impacted popular culture, phrases and quotes from the show began to spread into everyday conversation, especially for fans. Soon, almost anyone would know some of these quotes, whether or not they actually appeared on the show.

"Beam me up, Scotty."

Though no one ever actually said these exact words to Scotty, it's become accepted to mean, "Get me out of here."

"Live Long and Prosper."

Spock and other Vulcans often said this as a greeting or farewell and it was actually the proper response to someone saying "Peace and long life." Now abbreviated on social media as #LLAP

"Fascinating."

Spock's dry delivery of one or two words of dialogue could make it into a catchphrase. "Logical" or "Most illogical" also come from Spock.

"He's dead, Jim." "I'm a doctor, not a . . ."

McCoy, TOS

"Hailing frequencies open."

Uhura, TOS

"Engage."

Picard, TNG

"Make it so."

Picard, TNG

"Resistance is futile."

The Borg, TNG

"KHAAAAAN!"

Kirk, *Star Trek II: The Wrath of Khan*/ Spock, *Star Trek Into Darkness*

213

POPULAR POP-CULTURE
REFERENCES

YOUNG *STAR TREK* FANS GROW UP, AND SOME OF THEM BECOME SCIENTISTS, ACTORS, SINGERS, OR TV AND FILM PRODUCERS. EVEN AS SCIENTISTS BRING SOME OF *STAR TREK*'S TECHNOLOGY TO LIFE, ENTERTAINERS PAY HOMAGE OR INCORPORATE INSIDE JOKES INTO THEIR OWN WORKS, ASSIMILATING EVEN MORE OF THE GENERAL PUBLIC INTO THE WORLD OF *STAR TREK*. SOME OF THE MOST FAMOUS *STAR TREK* POP-CULTURE REFERENCES INCLUDE:

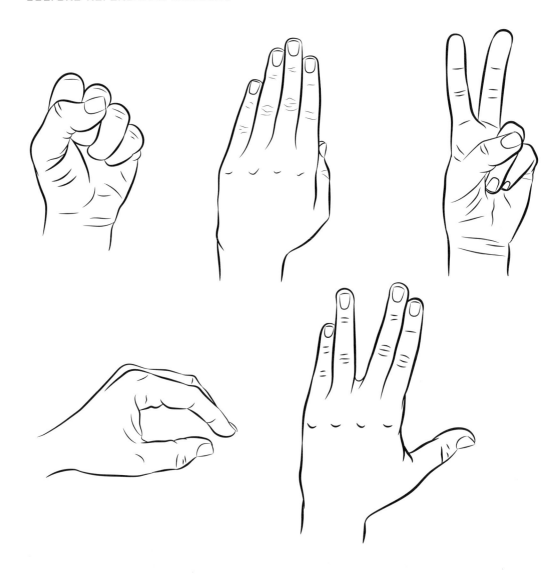

The Big Bang Theory The popular television sitcom has an ongoing love affair with *Star Trek*. The show's characters speak Klingon, debate the merits of the films and episodes, dress up like Starfleet officers and play games like Klingon Boggle and Rock-Paper-Scissors-Lizard-Spock.

Family Guy Creator Seth MacFarlane is a huge *Star Trek* fan and not only placed references throughout his series, he also reunited *The Next Generation* actors to provide voices for an episode where Stewie kidnapped the cast.

Galaxy Quest This film was a satirical look at what might happen if the actors from a *Star Trek*-like television show encountered real aliens.

Boston Legal William Shatner co-starred in the legal comedy/drama and references to *Star Trek* often appeared in dialogue. When his character received a cell phone as a gift, flipping it open made the same chirp sound as a communicator in The Original Series.

Gilmore Girls With its fast-talking characters dropping pop culture references at warp speed, it should be no surprise that *Star Trek* was mentioned over a dozen times during the series.

South Park The long-running series parodied numerous episodes of *Star Trek*, including "Miri," "Mirror, Mirror" and "Dagger of the Mind," and it once had a student wearing a red shirt be the first one to be killed by a monster.

Memes Captain Picard memes are especially well known, including the facepalm GIF and "annoyed Picard" memes.

Redshirts: A Novel with Three Codas This science-fiction novel by John Scalzi played off the trope of expendable characters in fiction, with a clear nod to The Original Series.

Pop Songs *Star Trek* references have popped up in pop music numerous times over the decades. Some of the most popular include Nena's "99 Luftballons," Red Hot Chili Peppers' "Californication," Semisonic's "Never You Mind," and the Weeknd's "Starboy." The Beastie Boys are among the top pop groups that paid tribute to the series with lyrics in both "Intergalactic" and "The Brouhaha," as well as some *Star Trek* cosplay in the video for "Ch-Check it Out." But few have celebrated *Star Trek* in their lyrics more than Weird Al Yankovic has in his song parodies.

Castle The mystery series celebrated pop culture as much as it solved murders, and it referenced *Star Trek* numerous times, including an episode entitled "The Final Frontier" that parodied *Star Trek* fandom and included an appearance by Armin Shimerman.

Bill & Ted's Bogus Journey Numerous films and television shows have either used footage from *Star Trek* or referenced the series, but not only did this popular film have its characters watching Kirk fight the Gorn from "Arena," they were later taken to Vasquez Rocks, where the original Gorn fight footage was shot and pushed to their doom by their evil robot duplicates.

LIST #99

ENTERTAINMENT MILESTONES

THE *STAR TREK* SHOWS BROKE MANY BARRIERS DURING EACH RUN, WITH MANY OF THEM BECOMING MILESTONE MOMENTS IN ENTERTAINMENT.

First adult American science-fiction show

While other science-fiction shows had appeared on television most were either aimed at families like *Lost In Space* or were anthology shows like *The Twilight Zone*. *Star Trek* was the first with a continuing cast with plots aimed at adults, focusing on the social issues of the day.

First show to be saved from cancellation by a letter-writing campaign

The Original Series was to be canceled after its second season. A massive fan-driven letter-writing campaign that some figures put at over a million letters—but NBC claimed officially 116,000— helped the show survive one more season.

First successful science-fiction show spinoff

Even discounting *The Animated Series*, *Star Trek: The Next Generation* was the first successful spinoff television series from a science-fiction program.

First American scripted interracial kiss on TV

Kirk and Uhura's kiss in "Plato's Stepchildren" had the network executives worried. While some kisses between Caucasian and Hispanic or Asian performers had been seen, none between an African American and Caucasian had been seen in a scripted television show before.

NASA names space shuttle after *U.S.S. Enterprise*

Another letter-writing campaign convinced NASA to name a shuttle after the *Enterprise*. White House officials sent a memo to President Gerald Ford saying NASA received hundreds of thousands of letters from *Star Trek* fans, and that the name had a naval tradition. On Sept. 17, 1976, the shuttle was dedicated at a ceremony with Gene Roddenberry and much of the original cast on hand.

LIST #100 FAMOUS STAR TREK FANS

For years, it seemed, *Star Trek* fans were on the fringes of fandom. Outside of conventions, the days of proudly wearing an "I Grok Spock" pin seemed to be in the past. *Star Trek: The Next Generation* and the films revitalized the franchise and suddenly, fans everywhere proclaimed their love of all things Trek including big-name celebrities.

President Barack Obama Not only did President Obama give the Vulcan salute when taking a photo with Nichelle Nichols, but he spoke to *Wired* magazine about watching *Star Trek* over and over as a child and how the optimism and values of the show talked about a theme of our common humanity.

Ben Stiller Actor/director Stiller uses many *Star Trek* references in his films and owns two pairs of Leonard Nimoy's Spock ears and other original *Star Trek* artifacts. Perhaps most telling, his production company is named after the Red Hour in The Original Series episode "The Return of the Archons."

Daniel Craig One actor behind the most famous secret agent of all once confessed to a secret ambition: a film role on *Star Trek*.

Tom Hanks Superstar actor Hanks competed with Simon Pegg on the British *Graham Norton Show* in a game of *Star Trek* trivia. He told Pegg he was ready to play a peaceful Romulan, should one appear in the new films.

Rihanna The pop singer not only contributed to the *Star Trek Beyond* soundtrack, but also explained in a promotional trailer for the single that her father introduced her to the show as a child and she felt emotionally connected to the *Enterprise* crew.

Mila Kunis From *That 70s Show* to the twenty-fourth century, actress Mila Kunis loves all things *Star Trek*, but lists her favorite as *The Next Generation*. Fellow fan Jason Segal from *How I Met Your Mother* once gave Kunis vintage *Star Trek* figures as a gift.

President Ronald Reagan After leaving Washington, the former actor and former president visited his old Hollywood stomping grounds while *The Next Generation* was in production. Though he was admittedly not a huge fan of *Star Trek*, when his diaries from his time in office were released to the public, it was revealed that it did have a private screening of *Star Trek III: The Search for Spock* in the White House movie theater. (He was not impressed.)

Brad Paisley The country music superstar is a huge sci-fi fan, with a special love for *Star Trek*. He became friends with both William Shatner and Zachary Quinto. Paisley even mashed up an acoustic version of the *Star Trek* and *Star Wars* themes on a radio show.

Seth MacFarlane The creator of *Family Guy* adds in *Star Trek* and other pop-culture references in his shows and films frequently. He also managed to "beam in" Captain Kirk when MacFarlane hosted the 2013 Academy Awards ceremony.

Rosario Dawson The actress lobbied on Twitter for a part in *Star Trek Into Darkness*, but ultimately wasn't cast in the film. She did prove that she was ready for a part as one of the most famous *Star Trek* aliens by speaking some Klingon on Conan O'Brien's talk show.

Dr. Martin Luther King, Jr. After the first season of The Original Series wrapped, actress Nichelle Nichols was preparing to leave the role of Uhura and join a show headed for Broadway. However, Dr. King sought her out at a fund-raiser to tell her what a fan he was and to urge her to stay on the show and continue to represent and inspire equality for all people.

THE LIST OF LISTS

ABOUT THE AUTHOR

Chip Carter began his trek into the written world with numerous *Star Trek* trading cards. After selling a story pitch to *Star Trek: Voyager*, he wrote the *Obsessed with Star Trek* trivia book, a trio of gift books highlighting *Star Trek* technology, and continues to work on other licensed products, including thousands of Trivial Pursuit questions for *The Walking Dead*, *Harry Potter*, and *Star Trek*.

ACKNOWLEDGMENTS

If you're writing a book, there is always a list of people to thank, and since this is a Book of Lists, here is an extra-special, no-added-cost Bonus List!

Thanks to the following at

BECKER&MAYER!

Scott Richardson

Farley Bookout

Olivia Holmes

Paul Ruditis, leader of the most Charmed life I know
(he will probably cut this!)

HARPERDESIGN

Marta Schooler

Lynne Yeamans

CBS

My old arch-nemesis, John Van Citters

My ally in Tuvixness, Marian Cordry

My most respected admiral, Risa Kessler

My favorite Trek tweeter, Holly Amos